WHAT I WISH I'D KNOWN

BEFORE MY MISSION

JOHN BYTHEWAY

DESERET BOOK COMPANY
SALT LAKE CITY, UTAH

*To my missionary hero, Abinadi, who may have felt that
he had failed as a missionary, but who through Alma the Elder
and his posterity altered the religious life of the Nephites
and Lamanites for more than five centuries*

© 1996 John Bytheway

Library of Congress Cataloging-in-Publication Data

Bytheway, John, 1962–
    What I wish I'd known before my mission / by John Bytheway.
      p.   cm.
    Includes bibliographical references and index.
    ISBN 1-57345-207-6 (pbk.)
    1. Church of Jesus Christ of Latter-day Saints—Missions—
Handbooks, manuals, etc. 2. Mormons—Missions—Handbooks, manuals,
etc. 3. Missionaries—Handbooks, manuals, etc. I. Title.
BX8661.B87   1996
266'.9332—dc20
                                      96-34139
                                        CIP

Printed in the United States of America   72082-4700
10   9

Contents

Acknowledgments

I wish to thank many people who have influenced this project. Special thanks go to my mission presidents, the late Elder Robert E. Sackley and President Menlo F. Smith, and to all my companions and fellow missionaries in the Philippines Baguio Mission.

I am also indebted to Russ and Colleen Peterson (and their fax machine), Kathy Schlendorf, Brad Wilcox, and Cameron Burrup for their helpful input and suggestions on the manuscript. Thanks also to Sheri Dew, Emily Watts, Shauna Gibby, and the entire Deseret Book staff.

Finally, thanks to my new wife, the former Kimberly Ann Loveridge, not only for marrying me (and thereby dramatically reducing the stress level of my parents) but also for giving me her constant encouragement and support.

PART ONE
Before You Go

*Remember that "it is a day of warning,
and not a day of many words."
If they receive not your testimony in one
place, flee to another, remembering to cast
no reflections, nor throw out any bitter
sayings. If you do your duty, it will
be just as well with you, as though
all men embraced the Gospel.*

—Teachings of the Prophet Joseph Smith, *p. 43*

Now What?

Some are better prepared to serve the Lord the first month in the mission field than some who are returning home after twenty-four months. We want young men entering the mission field "on the run." —President Ezra Taft Benson[1]

So, you've rented that cap and gown thing, you've walked down the aisle, and now you're a high school graduate, huh? Good for you! Now what? Well, now you wear shorts, sit around, guzzle pop, and watch ESPN. Right? Wrong! Well, okay, maybe for a day or two, but take another look at the program they passed out at graduation. You might notice another word on there: *Commencement.* To "commence" is to start. Graduation isn't the end, it's just the beginning! Your life is just getting started, my friend.

Up until now, you've been like a train. All you've had to do was follow the track. In sixth grade, if someone had asked you what you were doing with your life, you would have said, "huh?" because you were just following the track, doing what everyone else was doing. The track took you through elementary school, junior high, and high

3

school. Now, suddenly, the track ends. You've grown out of your choo-choo train, and now you can trade it in for an airplane that will take you anywhere you want to go.

So, what are your plans? Airplanes need flight plans, you know. If you're a young man, this is easy. If you're a young woman, it gets a little more interesting. I'll explain:

If you're a young man:
when you're 12, you're a deacon,
when you're 14, you're a teacher,
when you're 16, you're a priest,
when you're 19, you go on a mission,
when you're 21, you come home,
eventually get married, and live happily ever after . . .

If you're a young woman:
when you're 12, you're a Beehive,
when you're 14, you're a Mia Maid,
when you're 16, you're a Laurel,
when you're 18, you graduate,
and then . . .

Hey, what happened? You graduate from high school, and your world is wide open. You have more options than the young men of the same age. The prophets have said that every young man should serve a mission. But if you're a young woman, and you want to serve, you have a few more years to wait. What should you do? I'm glad you asked.

This may seem like a strange time to retell the story of David and Goliath, but stay tuned. When David was preparing to meet Goliath, he "chose him five smooth stones out of the brook" and put them in his bag (1 Samuel 17:40). Later, when he confronted Goliath, he "put his hand in his bag, and took thence a stone" (verse 49). The first stone he picked and hurled with his sling was the next thing that went through Goliath's head, so to speak.

You know the story, but here's a question you may never have thought of before. What if David had missed? What if his stone had flown over Goliath's head? Well, he had four other stones in his bag, and he would have loaded one of them. You see, *David had backup plans.* He had Plan A, Plan B, Plan C, Plan D, and Plan E.

Young women can do the same thing David did. You've graduated, and you are faced with a huge Goliath called "What should I do next?" Perhaps you want to go on a mission. Good for you! Reach in your bag, pull out the first stone, and label it *Plan A: Mission.* But wait! While you're preparing for Plan A, what if Mister Wonder—, I mean, *Brother* Wonderful comes along? Aha! Here's why you have five stones. You reach into your bag and label another stone *Plan B: Marriage,* you put it in your sling, and you bean him on the noggin. In the meantime, I suggest putting *Plan C: Education* in your sling while you're waiting to turn twenty-one.

If you're a young man, Plan A is a full-time mission, and that's the only stone you'll need right now. But you too might have to wait for a while before you can turn in your papers. What should you do?

Guy or girl, the important thing is that you have a purpose, a goal, an objective. Snarfing pizza and root beer while rotting in front of the TV is not a purpose. It's a lack of purpose. So, what kind of purpose should you have while preparing for a mission? Wait! We just missed it. Preparing for a mission *is* the purpose! That's the main thing. What are you doing? You're preparing—that's your purpose. Let's talk about how you can fulfill that purpose.

TIME TO PRESS "PAUSE" ON THE
TAPE RECORDER OF LOVE

Young women, this next part is for the guys—you already know what to do if Brother Wonderful comes along, right? Still got that rock in your bag? Okay. Young men, while preparing for a mission, you don't want to get your feet entangled in the anchor chain of the Love Boat.

The kind of girl you want to date and marry will not only want you to go on a mission, she will expect you to. She'll know that a mission can make you a much better person, and she won't be so selfish as to keep you from going.

One of my favorite definitions of a friend comes from Elder Robert D. Hales: "A true friend makes it easier to live the gospel."[2] At this time in a young man's life, living the gospel means going on a mission. The prophets have said it for years. If a romance is making it harder for you to go, you might have to ask, "Is this relationship a friend or an enemy?"

I'm not going to make fun of your feelings, or call them "puppy love." I know that those bonds of friendship and love can be very strong. This is just one of those times when you have to be tough and believe that God will take care of things. You've heard this verse before, but now you'll have to put it to the test: "Trust in the Lord with all thine heart; and lean not unto thine own understanding" (Proverbs 3:5).

Go ahead and date, but keep your mind on your purpose. Keep dates fun, keep them casual, and stay focused on your mission. We'll talk more about this later. Young women (I know you're still reading 'cause you saw the word *romance* in here), if Brother Wonderful comes along, you know what to do. Stay close to the Lord, your parents, and your bishop, *and keep your sling handy.*

INCREASE YOUR GOSPEL KNOWLEDGE

Here's a great way to prepare: Why not increase your gospel knowledge? I knew many missionaries who had read the Book of Mormon only once—if that—before they entered the Missionary Training Center. Don't let that be you. Read the Book of Mormon again, *keeping in mind the idea that you will be teaching it to others.* That will change your whole frame of mind. Identify the things that most impress you, the ones that make you feel different inside. When you sit across the room from your investigators, you want to be able to tell them that you have read the Book of Mormon carefully and that if they read it, they will have spiritual experiences similar to yours.

President Benson taught, "There is a difference between a convert who is built on the Rock of Christ through the Book of Mormon and stays hold of that rod of iron, and one who is not."[3] All by itself, the Book of Mormon is one of the most powerful tools in converting people to the gospel of Jesus Christ. My mission president was a very successful businessman and a great leader. But ten years before he was my mission president, he wasn't even a member of the Church. He was converted by the Book of Mormon. A copy had been sitting on a shelf in his home for many years. One day he decided to pick it up and start reading. After a short time, he said, "There's something to this book." He began to be convinced that it was deep, profound, and full of eternal truths and principles, and he began investigating the Church. Did missionaries knock on his door? No. Did members invite him over for family home evening? No. Did he see an ad on TV about the Church? No. He just picked up this wonderful book. If the Book of Mormon can do all that by itself, imagine what can happen if we add all the rest! You must be able to convince your investigators to read the Book of Mormon, and how can you do that unless you've carefully read it your-self?

Let me suggest some other books, too: *Gospel Principles* is a simple but thorough discussion of basic principles of the gospel. *Our Search for Happiness,* by Elder M. Russell Ballard, is a tenderly written book intended largely for investigators that will give you an idea of how to tactfully approach many subjects. I would also suggest you read James E. Talmage's classic *Jesus the Christ,* and *A Marvelous Work and a Wonder* by LeGrand Richards. These books will help you better understand the Savior's mission and will increase your testimony. All of these books are on the approved list for missionaries. Read them while you pre-pare!

DISCIPLINE YOURSELF

Weak discipline makes weak missionaries. The word *dis-cipline* sounds a lot like the word *disciple.* Being a disciple means being disciplined. On a mission you will have to discipline your eyes, your tongue, your mind, your whole body. Why not get started now?

A favorite quote of mine from President Gordon B. Hinckley has to do with discipline:

> One of the great tragedies we witness almost daily, is the tragedy of [missionaries] of high aim and low achievement. Their motives are noble, their pro-claimed ambition is praiseworthy, their capacity is great. But their discipline is weak. They succumb to indolence. Appetite robs them of will.[4]

Whenever I hear that quote, I think of how awful it would be to have President Hinckley look at me in the next life and say, "What a tragedy! You had high aim, but low achievement! Your motives were noble, your pro-claimed ambition was praiseworthy, and your capacity was great! *But your discipline was weak.* Your appetites robbed you of will." Yuck. Wouldn't that be awful? I don't want my discipline to be weak, or my appetites to rob my will. What appetites? The appetite for sleep, for example. You get tired on a mission like you do here at home. But the mission rules say early to bed and early to rise. Before I entered the MTC, I decided to get disciplined. I started going to bed early and getting up at 6:30 A.M. That way, it wasn't a big shock to my system when I entered the MTC.

What other appetites? How about the appetite for doing nothing, hanging around, or being lazy? Your discipline can overcome these appetites, too. A few years ago, I decided to stop watching TV for a month. You might want to try this; it's amazing what you can accomplish when you stop using the "plug-in drug." I believe that one of the reasons missionaries feel much more spiritual on their missions is because they stop spending hours vegging out in front of the tube. Think of what would happen in the Church if every member traded one half-hour TV show a day for a half-hour of scripture study!

There are other appetites, too. Rather than wait for me to try to point them out, why not just look inside your own heart? Are there any habits there that you'd like to change? You know better than anyone the things you could overcome with a little discipline. I am challenged by the statement of Robert Louis Stevenson: "You cannot run away from weakness. You must sometime fight it out or perish; and if that be so, why not now, and where you stand?" This is a perfect time to conquer the weaknesses you've been putting off fighting. Why not conquer them now and leave them in the dust when you go on your mission? Remember what the Lord taught about weakness (see Ether 12:27). Let him help you make weak things strong.

DEVELOP CHARITY

Another way to prepare for missionary service is to learn to love people. I don't know who said it, but throughout my mission I would repeat to myself this little phrase: "Every person is my superior in at least one way." I met and taught people in the Philippines who had less education at the age of fifty than I'd had when I was six. But if I'd had to compete with them in a rice farming contest, I would have gotten creamed. Others I met had seemingly infinite patience and Christlike meekness and humility. When I saw the kind of adversity these people endured, when the most impressive part of the Church they'd ever seen was my flip chart, it would humble me to tears. Perhaps some were uneducated and wore ragged clothes, but they were my superiors in *many* ways. Although we were very different, I learned to love them with my whole soul.

The Prophet Joseph Smith said: "Sectarian priests cry out concerning me, and ask, 'Why is it this babbler gains so many followers, and retains them?' I answer, It is because I possess the principle of love. All I can offer the world is a good heart and a good hand."[5]

Right now you might be impatient with people, especially some in your own family. Believe me, some of the people you'll miss the very most when you go on your mission are your family members. Parents say that one of the great changes that occurs in missionaries is in how they treat their families when they return.

You'll grow to love your family more and more. Hopefully, they are easy to love. One of the challenges of a mission—and of life in general—is to love those who are hard to love, even "perishing souls." Joseph Smith taught:

Nothing is so much calculated to lead people to forsake sin as to take them by the hand, and watch over them with tenderness. When persons manifest the least kindness and love to me, O what power it has over my mind, while the opposite course has a tendency to harrow up all the harsh feelings and depress the human mind. . . .

The nearer we get to our heavenly Father, the more we are disposed to look with compassion on perishing souls; we feel that we want to take them upon our shoulders, and cast their sins behind our backs.[6]

Prime time has not taught us much of charity. Most of what we see is one put-down after another. The world has taught us to be judgmental and sarcastic. That won't work on a mission. Charity will work, because *charity never faileth!* (See Moroni 7:46.)

CONTROL YOUR THOUGHTS

Ralph Waldo Emerson once said, "A man is what he thinks about all day long." If that were literally true, a lot of young men would have turned into girls a long time ago. Seriously, though, if we can control our thoughts, we can control what we become.

On a mission, it's not easy to keep your thoughts focused on the work. There are many other thoughts that would like to occupy your mind—thoughts of home, discouragement, or past romances. I never worked so hard to control my thoughts as I did on my mission. It's not easy! With so many outside influences, you have to vigorously defend your brain as if it were a plot of land. There will always be invaders, and you must try not to let them enter. If they do enter your land, you must chase them off, then turn around and be ready to defend again.

Earlier, I mentioned that you have to discipline even your eyes on a mission. I wasn't joking. In many countries, pornography is found in public places. Jesus said that we should "let virtue garnish [our] thoughts unceasingly" (D&C 121:45). That can be hard to do in a world that is obsessed with violence and immorality. I remember times on my mission when I would just stare at the floor, trying to focus my thoughts on spiritual things. You cannot run away and hide from the ugliness of the world, although sometimes that sounds like it might be nice. Your duty is to go into the world and let your light shine. When you keep your thoughts on the Savior, that light will come through. On occasion, people may even say that you seem to "glow."

Sometimes the thoughts you have to fight are not evil or unclean, they're just faithless. It's easy to have doubtful and fearful thoughts on your mission. The best way to ward off discouraging, fearful, or inappropriate thoughts is to replace them with something else. Jesus told us exactly how to do that: "Look unto me in every thought; doubt not, fear not" (D&C 6:36). *Every* thought. That's a pretty high percentage, isn't it? President Brigham Young said:

> If you go on a mission to preach the Gospel with lightness and frivolity in your hearts, looking for this and that, and to learn what is in the world, and not having your minds riveted—yes, I may say riveted— on the cross of Christ, you will go and return in vain. . . . Let your minds be centered on your missions and labor earnestly to bring souls to Christ.[7]

May I be so bold as to suggest that if you really want to prepare for your mission, and really prepare well, that you cut down on television, if not cut it out completely. Get started on those books I mentioned, and get your mind on the task before you. I know that it's really nice sometimes to just pick up the remote and unwind in front of the set. But as I look back, I realize that watching TV hasn't really done much for me—it may have done more harm than good. Reading, on the other hand, has expanded my mind and exploded my testimony. If you can learn to enjoy reading as much as you do television, your whole life will change. When would you like your life to change? Well, why not now?

It looks like we're about done with this chapter. You've graduated, but your life is just about to "commence." Use these months and years before it's time to turn in your papers to get ready for the adventure of a lifetime—your mission. Date casually, increase your gospel knowledge, discipline yourself, develop charity, and learn to better control your thoughts.

All of this ought to keep you busy until it's time to turn in your papers. First, though, you might want to finish this book. So here's what we're going to do: we'll talk about getting your call, and mention a couple of things you should *not* worry about. In Part Two, we'll visit the MTC and give you some ideas about what to expect. We'll talk about mission life, work habits, and potential distractions. We'll look to Ammon for some powerful principles of missionary work, followed by a word about the importance of keeping the mission rules. In Part Three, we'll put it all together in a discussion of "the Lord, my companion, and me." After that, an appendix is included to help you see the big picture and gain a better understanding of the Restoration.

Ready to move on? Good. Go check your mailbox, and I'll see you in the next chapter.

---

1. *Teachings of Ezra Taft Benson* (Salt Lake City: Bookcraft, 1988), p. 192.
2. *Ensign*, May 1990, p. 40.

3. *Ensign,* May 1975, p. 65.

4. *Ensign,* May 1979, p. 65.

5. *Teachings of the Prophet Joseph Smith,* sel. Joseph Fielding Smith (Salt Lake City: Deseret Book, 1976), p. 313.

6. *Teachings of the Prophet Joseph Smith,* pp. 240–241.

7. *Discourses of Brigham Young,* comp. John A. Widtsoe (Salt Lake City: Deseret Book, 1975), p. 325.

A Letter from the Prophet

I promise you that the time you spend in the mission field, if those years are spent in dedicated service, will yield a greater return on investment than any other two years of your lives. —President Gordon B. Hinckley[1]

I don't know about you, but I don't get a whole lot of mail from the prophet. But one day, he sent me a letter—a letter I'd been waiting for all my life. I'd heard lessons about it, and sung songs about it, and on this day, it came. *It came to pass!* It will happen to you too.

When you read "Office of the First Presidency" on the return address, it causes several biological changes in your system. You get the chills, your heart races, and your hands shake with anticipation.

The day my letter came, someone else had brought the mail in, and it was sitting on the usual place on the table. My younger sister and I were the only ones home. I wanted to open my letter by myself, so I grabbed it and ran downstairs to the privacy of my basement bedroom. I dropped to my knees. "Heavenly Father," I began, "I don't care where I go, just please let me know in my heart that it's right." I closed my prayer and carefully opened the letter.

"Dear Elder Bytheway: You are hereby called to serve as a missionary of The Church of Jesus Christ of Latter-day Saints to labor in the Philippines Baguio Mission . . ." *The Philippines! Wow, how wonderful! How exciting! How exotic! Where are the Philippines?* I ran upstairs, shouted "The Philippines!" to my sister, and dashed to the encyclopedia, thoughts racing through my head. *Tropical islands, I think . . . wow, I bet it's hot and humid, I'll probably wear short-sleeved shirts. . . .* I found a map of the Philippines—a place I would come to know and love like the back of my hand. I looked for the city of Baguio. *How in the world do you say* Baguio? *Buh-gwi? Buh-gyo? Buh-goo-ee-oh?* There it was, in the mountains of an island called Luzon. I would get to know that map and the accompanying article very well in the next few weeks.

The day you get "the call" is one you'll never forget. How will it be for you? "Did you get anything in the mail today, dear?" Mom asks dutifully. "Nothin' really, Mom," you reply, "just a letter from the prophet . . ." "That's nice dea . . . WHAT!?" she says as the silverware in her hands drops to the floor. "Yeah, the prophet needs a little assistance in the field. I need to take off for a while and do a little thrashing."

> Wherefore, I call upon the weak things of the world, those who are unlearned and despised, to thrash the nations by the power of my spirit. (D&C 35:13)

YOUR CALL IS INSPIRED

How about you? Are you just doing a little reading while you wait for your call to come, or have you gotten it already? Well, even if you haven't, you have. You were called a long time ago, and so was I. The Prophet Joseph Smith said:

> Every man who has a calling to minister to the inhabitants of the world was ordained to that very purpose in the Grand Council of heaven before this world was. I suppose that I was ordained to this very office in that Grand Council.[2]

So maybe we don't *get* a mission call, maybe we're just *reminded* of our call by the prophet. The signature on my letter from the First Presidency said, "Spencer W. Kimball." President Kimball "reminded" me of my call, as the prophets today remind many others. Was my call inspired? I know it was. President Thomas S. Monson relates:

> On one occasion I remember having read the detail on a particular missionary candidate, and President Kimball indicated that the young man would go, I believe, to London, England. Then he said, "No. That is not correct. Send the young man to the Denmark Copenhagen Mission." I looked on the form and noticed that I had overlooked reading a very important statement from the stake president. I said, "President Kimball, have you ever seen this form before?" "No," he replied. "Look at what the stake president has written," I continued. "The grandfather of this missionary candidate is an immigrant from the land of Denmark. He is our stake patriarch. The missionary candidate was promised in his patriarchal blessing that if he lived true and faithful he would return to the land of his forbears, that he might preach the gospel in that particular land." President Kimball nodded his approval and said, "The Lord's will has been made known today."[3]

Perhaps one of the purposes of having living prophets

on the earth is to *remind* us of our past, who we are, and what we should be. They remind us that we fought in the war in heaven. And the "weapons" we used were faith and testimony. The fact that you are here on earth is proof that you followed the Father's plan and were victorious. And now, as further evidence of your faith, you're going on a mission to share your testimony with others.

SOME THINGS *NOT* TO WORRY ABOUT

Normal doubts and fears may arise as you approach your time as a full-time missionary. Some of the most common are the fear that you don't have a strong enough testimony, the fear that you won't be very good at talking to people, and the fear of learning a new language.

Is my testimony strong enough? To be completely honest, this was one of my fears. I just wasn't sure I could go out and look people in the eye and tell them, "I know this is true," when I wasn't sure if I knew. I *believed* it, and I *wanted* it to be true, but I wasn't as sure as I thought I was supposed to be. But I decided to move ahead, following the example of Nephi. Remember how Lehi asked Nephi to return to Jerusalem and get the brass plates from Laban? Nephi didn't know exactly how he was going to do it, but he went anyway. "And I was led by the Spirit, not knowing beforehand the things which I should do" (1 Nephi 4:6). I decided I would go to the MTC, "not knowing beforehand" all I wanted to know, but trusting that God would help me.

I did go. And I spent many hours in the custodial closets at night praying for a testimony. I found privacy next to the vacuum cleaners and the brooms, and I prayed my heart out every night I could for several nights. I didn't get anything. At least not in the MTC.

That personal witness did come soon after I arrived in the Philippines. The details are not important, but the

Lord made it very clear to me that I already had a testimony. He helped me to see that I had felt the Spirit all my life; I just didn't recognize it as such. I learned how really subtle the "still, small voice" can be, and how the little things we do can affect our ability to recognize it.

Another critically important lesson I learned is that we have to *act* before we can receive the answers. God cannot steer a parked car. This principle should have been obvious to me—I'd gone to church all my life—but somehow it took my mission to open my eyes and engrave it on my soul. I found, as I'm sure you will too, that the Spirit often waits until you are bearing your testimony before it comes.

It is one of the most wonderful experiences you'll ever have to be testifying in faith of what you believe to be true, and then have the Spirit whisper in that very moment, "What you are saying right now is true." The Spirit didn't say to me before I taught, "What you are *about* to teach is true"; it always seemed to wait until I was bearing testimony, and then it would tell me that I was teaching absolute truth. Later in my mission, I came across what may be the most important quote in this book. Just reading it strengthened my testimony. What Elder Boyd K. Packer said confirmed everything I had recently learned for myself:

> It is not unusual for a missionary to say, "How can I bear testimony until I get one? How can I testify that God lives, that Jesus is the Christ and that the gospel is true? If I do not have such a testimony would not that be dishonest?"
>
> Oh, if I could teach you this one principle! A testimony is to be *found* in the *bearing* of it. Somewhere in your quest for spiritual knowledge, there is that "leap of faith," as the philosophers call it. It is the moment when you have gone to the edge of the light and step

into the darkness to discover that the way is lighted ahead for just a footstep or two. The spirit of man, as the scripture says, indeed is the candle of the Lord.

It is one thing to receive a witness from what you have read or what another has said; and that is a necessary beginning. It is quite another to have the Spirit confirm to you in your bosom that what *you* have testified is true. Can you not see that it will be supplied as you share it? As you give that which you have, there is a replacement, with increase!⁴

If you are wondering if your testimony is strong enough for you to serve a mission, take my advice and go. Take that step of absolute faith. Go! Move forward, and allow the Lord to confirm that what you are doing is right. Remember, "Ye receive no witness until after the trial of your faith" (Ether 12:6). Act first, and the confirmation will come. With Elder Packer, I testify, *a testimony is found in the bearing of it!*

I'm not very good at talking to people. Here's another thing not to worry about. If you feel this way, you're in great company. The Lord doesn't call people to be missionaries because they are great public speakers. Let's look at a couple of examples. When Moses was called to lead the children of Israel out of bondage, he responded, "O my Lord, I am not eloquent, neither heretofore, nor since thou hast spoken unto thy servant: but I am slow of speech, and of a slow tongue." The Lord answered him, "Now therefore go, and I will be with thy mouth, and teach thee what thou shalt say" (Exodus 4:10, 12).

Enoch was called to tell the people to repent. He worried, "Why is it that I have found favor in thy sight, and am but a lad, and all the people hate me; for I am slow of speech" (Moses 6:31). The Lord answered, "Go forth and do as I have commanded thee, and no man shall pierce thee. Open thy mouth, and it shall be filled, and I will give thee utterance, for all flesh is in my hands, and I will do as seemeth me good" (Moses 6:32). Isn't it interesting that, in both cases, the Lord answered with the word "go!" The Spirit is the key. President Brigham Young taught:

> With regard to preaching, let a man present himself before the Saints, or go into the world before the nobles and great men of the earth, and let him stand up full of the Holy Ghost, full of the power of God, and though he may use words and sentences in an awkward style, he will convince and convert more, of the truth, than can the most polished orator destitute of the Holy Ghost; for that Spirit will prepare the minds of the people to receive the truth, and the spirit of the speaker will influence the hearers so that they will feel it.[5]

J. Elliot Cameron expressed the same idea in three words: *Inspiration supersedes talent!* The fact is, you don't have to be good at talking to people to be an effective missionary—you just have to have the Spirit of the Lord. And since being humble and recognizing your dependence on the Lord is absolutely necessary to qualify for spiritual help, being slow of speech might just be an advantage! I could name a couple of missionaries in my mission who could best be described as "slow of speech." One of them couldn't even read, but they were both wonderfully effective. They slowly bore simple testimonies, using simple words, and because of their humility and the presence of the Spirit, they brought many people to the truth. It humbled the more eloquent elders who heard them teach. If not being able to talk to people is one of your concerns, put your hand in the hand of the Lord and then open your mouth!

Open your mouths and they shall be filled, and you shall become even as Nephi of old, who journeyed from Jerusalem in the wilderness.

Yea, *open your mouths* and spare not, and you shall be laden with sheaves upon your backs, for lo, I am with you.

Yea, *open your mouths* and they shall be filled, saying: Repent, repent, and prepare ye the way of the Lord, and make his paths straight; for the kingdom of heaven is at hand. (D&C 33:8–10; emphasis added)

Elder Neal A. Maxwell has often repeated, "God does not begin by asking us about our ability, but only about our availability, and if we then prove our dependability, he will increase our capability!"[6] The Lord is more than able to help you reach your full potential. Whenever I felt afraid to talk to people on my mission—and I often did—I remembered this little verse: "The Lord is my light and my salvation; whom shall I fear? the Lord is the strength of my life; of whom shall I be afraid?" (Psalm 27:1). With God on your side, you are an overwhelming majority.

I'm not sure I can learn another language. If this one scares you, that's good, because the only way you'll learn another language is to be humble enough to qualify for the Lord's help. With the Lord on your side, you can do it! And you can do it so fast it will startle you. Once again, your fear is normal and understandable. I love this story from President Thomas S. Monson:

When I served as chairman of the Church Missionary Committee . . . I received a telephone call from a member of the presidency of the Missionary Training Center at Provo, Utah. He advised that a particular young man assigned to a Spanish-speaking mission was having difficulty applying himself to his language study and had declared, "I never can learn

Spanish!" The leader asked, "What do you recommend we do?"

I thought for a moment, then suggested, "Place him tomorrow as an observer in a class of missionaries struggling to learn Japanese, and then advise me his reaction."

My caller responded within 24 hours with the report, "The missionary was only in the Japanese language class one-half day when he called me back and excitedly said, "Place me back in the Spanish class! I know I can learn that language." And he did.[7]

People from all over the world visit the MTC to figure out how our church can train missionaries so rapidly to speak other languages. They observe, they ask questions, and they take a lot of notes. But the one thing that doesn't usually end up on their notepads is the fact that the Lord is helping these young men and women. And why does he help them? Because he has a promise to keep:

> For it shall come to pass in that day, that every man shall hear the fulness of the gospel in his own tongue, and in his own language, through those who are ordained unto this power, by the administration of the Comforter, shed forth upon them for the revelation of Jesus Christ. (D&C 90:11)

You will be one of the Lord's instruments to help him keep that promise. What a privilege! Don't be discouraged if you leave the MTC not feeling fluent in your new language. You don't need to be fluent in the MTC van. When you are face-to-face with an investigator and you need to communicate, this is when the Lord will be there to help you "in the very moment" and give you what you should say (see D&C 100:6).

Overcoming your fears is an important part of your life

and growth, and a mission is the perfect place to overcome them. A mission will teach you, and strengthen you, and humble you, and refine you, and stretch you. (If you don't watch your diet, it will definitely stretch you.) My mission president used to call a mission a "short-cut to maturity." He also used to say, "The Lord gets the work done through his people, and his people 'done' through the work." When you return, there will be many people who will know more about Jesus Christ because you served. In addition, *you* will know a whole lot more about *you*. When my brother returned from his mission in Japan two months before I entered the MTC, he told me, "Your testimony will grow more than you imagine is possible." And he was right. I'm very excited for you, my friend. When you give your life to God, you allow him to bless you in ways you haven't dreamed of. President Ezra Taft Benson taught:

> Men and women who turn their lives over to God will discover that He can make a lot more out of their lives than they can. He will deepen their joys, expand their vision, quicken their minds, strengthen their muscles, lift their spirits, multiply their blessings, increase their opportunities, comfort their souls, raise up friends, and pour out peace. Whoever will lose his life in the service of God will find eternal life (see Matthew 10:39).[8]

You will never regret "turning your life over to God" by serving a mission. I cannot begin to tell you what my mission has meant to me. Next to my marriage, I consider it my most wonderful achievement. It was hard, it was long, it was exciting, and it was fun; it stretched me in every direction, it humbled me to tears, and it filled my heart with happiness and joy that made me want to run up and down the streets and shout the good news. I came to know the Lord, I learned how to pray, and I felt the Holy Ghost burn within me when I bore my testimony. At times I touched my hand to my chest to see if my shirt was on fire. I had never felt anything like that before. It was when I was on my mission that I discovered, *really* discovered the scriptures. I had read the scriptures before—hey, I was a seminary graduate. But on my mission the words of the ancient prophets seemed to leap off the page and scream in my ears. The Book of Mormon was so real! It became an adventure that I couldn't put down! I have been home for several years now, but I reflect on the events of my mission almost every day. Sometimes, knowing what I know now, I wish I could go back and do it over again. But I can't. So I'm doing the next best thing: sharing with you all these things I wish I'd known before I served my mission.

Although I plan to have some fun with you as we continue, I want you to know that I am extremely serious about this project. I've included quotes and principles and stories that helped me immeasurably as a missionary. I would have been a better elder had I known them sooner. My hope is that they will help you to be a more effective tool in the Lord's hands.

I wish there were a way that I could reach out through this book and meet you and shake your hand. I would be meeting one of the rarest young people in the world: someone willing to leave home and comfort and to go wherever you are called to go, to work and labor and teach the gospel of Jesus Christ. What a remarkable person you must be! You realize that it's time to "pay tithing" on your life, and the windows of heaven will most certainly open to you (see Malachi 4:10).

Do you know what to expect? Do you know what it will be like? I didn't. Some things I envisioned, and some I wouldn't ever have guessed. I can give you some ideas, but I'm not even going to attempt to teach you what they teach in the Missionary Training Center. They know what they're doing there, and they're better at it than I am. The MTC is a wonderful place, and you'll have many spiritual experiences there as you prepare to enter the mission field. I know, because I used to teach new missionaries there myself. So, are you ready to go? Good. Turn the page and I'll meet you at the Missionary Training Center!

---

1. *Ensign*, November 1995, p. 52.
2. *Teachings of the Prophet Joseph Smith*, sel. Joseph Fielding Smith (Salt Lake City: Deseret Book, 1976), p. 365.
3. *Ensign*, March 1996, p. 5.
4. Boyd K. Packer, *That All May Be Edified* (Salt Lake City: Bookcraft, 1982), pp. 339–40.
5. In *Journal of Discourses*, 26 vols. (London: Latter-day Saints' Book Depot, 1856–86), 4:21.
6. *Ensign*, July 1975, p. 7.
7. *Ensign*, May 1996, p. 44.
8. *Teachings of Ezra Taft Benson* (Salt Lake City: Bookcraft, 1988), p. 361.

PART TWO
In the Field

*I can promise you that the
Spirit is a lot more anxious to
help you than you are to be helped.*

—S. Dilworth Young

The Missionary Training Center

"MTC—24 hours a day until the sun goes out."
—Printed on a T-shirt at an LDS bookstore

Before we start, let's take a little quiz: What do these seventeen different countries have in common?

Argentina	Mexico
Brazil	New Zealand
Chile	Peru
Colombia	Philippines
Dominican Republic	Samoa
England	Spain
Guatemala	Tonga
Japan	United States
Korea	

The answer, believe it or not, is that they all have their own Missionary Training Centers! Did you know that? I didn't, until I called the MTC and asked. So maybe we shouldn't call this chapter "The Missionary Training Center," maybe we should call it "Your Missionary Training Center." For most of you who read this book, your MTC will be in Provo, Utah. Just keep in mind that there are MTCs all over the world. In fact, on February 26, 1996, the Church announced a "crossover." On that date the number of members of the Church outside the United States surpassed the number inside the United States. So we'll probably see even more MTCs around the globe in the future. Truly, we are a worldwide religion. And these MTCs are preparing the armies that will go into all the world with the good news of the gospel.

So welcome to your Missionary Training Center, one of the most incredible places on earth! There's no other place like an MTC. Can you think of anything similar in the world? Seriously, can you? Where else will you find thousands of dedicated young people preparing to go out into all parts of the world for no pay, every one of whom has volunteered to be there? Where else will you find such unity of purpose? But, most important to me, where else can you find the Spirit of the Lord in such abundance? One of my friends who left for his mission a few months before me told me in a letter, "Angels walk the halls in this place." I believe it. Next to the temple, the MTC is one of my favorite places on earth. It will be one of your favorite places too, and you will learn quickly that you need the help of the Spirit, and perhaps of angels, as you enter and get to work.

In the MTC, you'll share a room similar to one you might find in a college dorm. You'll have a companion, you'll have a branch, you'll have a branch president, you'll have a choir, you'll visit the temple once a week, you'll have physical exercise time, you'll have an MTC dance (just kidding), and you'll do some of the most intense learning you've ever done. You'll feel overwhelmed at the amount of material you're asked to master, and you'll be amazed that with the Lord's help you can actually do it. That last sentence went by really fast, so I think I'll repeat it for emphasis. *You will feel overwhelmed.* Did you get that? Every missionary I've ever known has made that comment about the MTC. That overwhelmed feeling is good, though, because it will help you realize how much you need the Lord. When you're feeling it, realize too that in the strength of the Lord, you can do all things (see Alma 26:12).

Anyway, back to the MTC. For the first couple of days you'll have several orientation meetings to let you know about your new routine. Eventually, you'll meet the teachers who will help you learn the discussions and, if necessary, the language. The teachers are returned missionaries who will spend many hours with you. You'll love them. And if you're smart, you'll listen to everything they tell you. They've been there, they've done it, and you would be wise to learn as much as you can from them. After my mission, I taught at the MTC, and I saw some ways new missionaries could make the most of their experience there.

ELIMINATING DISTRACTIONS

Because you are on the Lord's errand, the adversary will try to distract you. He'll use fear, feelings of inadequacy, homesickness, girlfriends or boyfriends, discouragement, and anything else he can think of. Don't let it happen! In the words of Joshua 1:9: "Have not I commanded thee? Be strong and of a good courage; be not afraid, neither be thou dismayed: for the Lord thy God is with thee whithersoever thou goest." Just being aware of the fact that Satan will try to distract you will help you as you get started.

Girlfriends and boyfriends. Okay, let's get right down to business and ask the big question: Is it okay to have a girlfriend or boyfriend at home while you're serving your mission? The best answer is a very definite maybe. In other words, it depends. It depends on your attitude as well as your friend's. Is the person a help or a hindrance? Does the relationship make you a better missionary or a worse one? If you are both careful about what you say in your letters, a girlfriend or boyfriend can actually be a help. But if you get gooey, reliving past dates or romantic experiences, it will be much harder for you to concentrate and keep your mind on the work. In my not-very-humble opinion (I feel rather strongly about this), the attitude to have when you leave for your mission is this: "I'm going to serve the Lord. I want to serve him with all my might, mind and strength, as the scriptures say I should. I know that if we both strive to keep the commandments and live the gospel, the Lord will take care of us both. If you are still here and available when I return, we can date and see how things work out. But I won't ask you to put your life on hold for me. If the Lord has something different in mind for either one of us, all we have to do is live the gospel and he will help us find it. In this way, if we both just strive to live the gospel, we can't lose."

Now, I know that if you are involved in a relationship you may be saying, "Yeah, right." Hey, I didn't say it was the easiest attitude! But I believe it is the best one.

If you're not careful, you can sour your whole mission experience by moping, worrying, and daydreaming about someone back home. When I was in the MTC, we had an elder in my building who had a virtual "shrine" on his desk of pictures and mementos of his girlfriend. He never made it into the mission field. His mind was so much on her, and so little on the work, that he couldn't progress. What a tragedy! What a waste! I plead with you, when you go to the MTC, jump in with both feet, with a whole-hearted, don't-look-back attitude. When it comes to that special someone you left behind, well, friend, it all comes down to good old-fashioned faith. You'll just have to exercise it. Be still and know that God is God, and all flesh is in his hands (see D&C 101:16). Have the faith that he will take care of you, and that he will "order all things for your good, as fast as ye are able to receive them" (D&C 111:11).

There is nothing that lovesick worrying can do for you. Nothing. Moping, worrying, and stewing accomplish nothing. They always lead to failure. What's worse, they distract you from the really important things that are going on. The opposite of worry is faith. "Look unto me in every thought; doubt not, fear not" (D&C 6:36). Remember those words whenever those lovesick feelings start creeping in, and say to yourself, "Faith, not fear. I will doubt not, and fear not. I will be still, and know that he is God."

Feeling homesick. Perhaps your mission will be one of the first times you've been away from home for very long. And you might miss home. I did, and so did lots of other missionaries I knew. Don't misunderstand what homesickness is. It's okay to miss home—Mom would probably be disappointed if you didn't. But *missing home* is a lot different from *wanting to quit and go home.*

There are many things you can do if you miss home. Let your gratitude and appreciation for your home grow, and let your love for your family grow, too. Just don't let those feelings occupy your mind for long periods of time. The best way to combat homesickness is to get lost in the work. Get a sense of purpose. Set some short-term goals about memorizing your discussions and scriptures. Reread your mission call and remember its promises. Get back to work and look ahead to the experience before you. Once again, doubting and fearing and thinking about home do not accomplish anything. Your home will be there when you return, and Mom's cooking will taste better . . . (Oops—I probably shouldn't mention Mom's cooking in a section about how not to feel homesick—sorry.) Um, what I mean is, home will be even better when you return after serving an honorable mission. You can do this! Hundreds of thousands already have! You know many returned missionaries in your home ward and stake, don't you? If they can do it, so can you!

I remember many missionaries who seemed to have a hard time getting both feet into the mission field. They were less effective than they could have been, and it was because they moped about home so much. I also noticed that these were the missionaries who seemed to have the hardest time adjusting once they returned home. All of a sudden, they longed for their mission again! The cure? I'll say it again—for best results, keep both feet in the same place. Plant both feet firmly in your mission field and get to work. Then, when you leave your mission field to return home, you'll know you did your best and it will be much easier to bring both feet home again and move on with your life.

MTC = "MAKE TIME COUNT"

One of the most important things that you can do in the MTC is to form work habits that will last for your entire mission. Decide that you are going to work hard on your mission. Decide that you will not count your time, but that instead you will make your time count. If I had only one message to give you about the MTC, this would be it: *Make time count.* Your time in one of the best places on earth is so short. Make the most of it. Use every minute. Learn all you can. In reality, because you are doing the Lord's work, your time becomes his time. Make it count!

We had a little saying in our mission: "You have two years to do it, and the rest of eternity to think about it." It's true. After you return home, you'll think about your mission nearly every day. Even while you're still on your mission, when you work hard, knowing you've done your best for the Lord, there's a great feeling of satisfaction when your head hits the pillow. You'll find that a good night's rest comes only after a good day's work. There will be few times in your life when you can go to your knees in prayer at the end of the day knowing without a doubt that you are exactly where the Lord wants you to be. I loved those times on my mission when I could say to the Lord in my personal prayers, "Father, we worked hard today," and I knew that he knew it was true.

Remember, Moses 1:39 begins, "For behold, this is my work . . . " Many young people have a bad taste in their mouths when they hear the word *work*. If that's true for you, you need some mental mouthwash. Work is not the enemy—it is your friend. Work is the antidote for depression. Work is part of the formula for success! President Ezra Taft Benson said:

> I have often said one of the greatest secrets of missionary work is work! If a missionary works, he will get the Spirit; if he gets the Spirit, he will teach by the Spirit; and if he teaches by the Spirit, he will touch the hearts of the people and he will be happy. There will be no homesickness, no worrying about families, for all time and talents and interests are centered on the work of the ministry. Work, work, work—there is no satisfactory substitute, especially in missionary work.[1]

You've heard all those stories about the legendary missionaries "from a farm in Idaho." What is it about those guys? I'll tell you. They know how to work. And missionaries who know how to work have great missions.

My parents taught me the value of work long before I was mission age, and I am thankful for that. But I will also always be grateful to Elder Charles E. Buckhannon III. He was my first companion when I arrived in the Philippines. Elder Buckhannon is not from Idaho, he's from Arizona, but he knows how to work. We worked hard, and the funny thing is that I didn't know we were working hard. Because I got used to using every minute wisely, never sleeping in or sitting around, those first work habits set a pattern for the rest of my mission. It was months later when I found out that not every missionary worked as hard as we did. I was surprised and disappointed in some of the others, but their attitude didn't change me a bit because I had already formed the work habits! So, to pass along Elder Buckhannon's example, I taught my new companions to work hard too (although of course I didn't tell them we were working hard).

President Henry D. Moyle, a former member of the First Presidency, said:

> I think if I have one accomplishment in life, I honestly and humbly believe it's to know how to work . . . . The hardest work I ever did was in the mission field; and the harder it seemed, the more I tried to do it . . . . I have never known the day when I was afraid to tackle the hardest stuff and do the best I could with them.
>
> I love to get up in the morning and after I have pondered over in my mind what I might do today that would be a little better than what I did yesterday, then be able to go out and have the courage, fortitude, and perseverance to overcome the obstacles that confront us in our work and accomplish that which we plan for ourselves. That is life and that is success!
>
> Let's work! I shall go to my grave saying that missionaries generally speaking never rise in their entire life above the stature they carve out for themselves in the mission field.[2]

I read that quotation before my mission, and it had a profound effect on me. Throughout my mission, I asked

myself, "What stature will I carve out for myself as a missionary? If my mission is going to set a pattern for my
life, what kind of life do I want? Do I want a moping,
homesick, half-hearted, one-footed, somewhat-obedient,
mediocre life? Or a determined, purposeful, energetic, full-
throttle, commandment-keeping, extraordinary life?" I
wanted the latter. And I thank my parents and Elder
Buckhannon for teaching me how to work.

If you don't know how to work, or if you don't like to
work, work anyway. You'll come to realize after a while
that, as with most things in life, you have a choice. You can
either enjoy work or despise it; it's up to you. To para-
phrase the words of Og Mandino, "You may work grudg-
ingly, or you may work gratefully. You may work as an
animal, or you may work as a man."3

My feelings about and my testimony of hard work came
to me while singing in a chapel in Baguio City, surrounded
by Filipino members and investigators. With all those
smiling, humble, happy people around me, singing their
hearts out, the words of the hymn jumped right off the
page and burned their place in my heart: "Sweet is the
work!"

MOVING ON . . .

Well, my friend, I'm not going to tell you much more
about the MTC. I want to encourage you to go there full of
anticipation and excitement. Remember there are sixteen
other MTCs in the world, and those elders and sisters are
battling their distractions too. They can do it, and so can
you! Think about these motivating words of Doctrine and
Covenants 4:1–4:

Now behold, a marvelous work is about to come
forth among the children of men.
Therefore, O ye that embark in the service of God,

see that ye serve him with all your heart, might, mind and strength, that ye may stand blameless before God at the last day.

Therefore, if ye have desires to serve God ye are called to the work;

For behold the field is white already to harvest; and lo, he that thrusteth in his sickle with his might, the same layeth up in store that he perisheth not, but bringeth salvation to his soul.

The MTC is the launching pad for the rest of your mission. So thrust in your sickle with all your might, make time count, and set a pattern for your mission and your future life by working hard. You'll love the MTC. But after you've been there for a while, you'll be downright antsy to get out and get to work. Then the real fun begins!

---

1. *Teachings of Ezra Taft Benson* (Salt Lake City: Bookcraft, 1988), p. 200.
2. "I'd Rather Be a Missionary . . ." (Central British Mission Publication, 1962). Cited in John D. Whetton, *Making the Most of Your Mission* (Salt Lake City: Deseret Book, 1981), p. 18.
3. Og Mandino, *The Greatest Secret in the World* (New York: Bantam Books, 1981), p. 66.

Called to Serve

Lift up your heart and rejoice, for the hour of your mission is come; and your tongue shall be loosed, and you shall declare glad tidings of great joy unto this generation. —D&C 31:3

Now that you're out in the field, what do you do? Well, if you need an example of a successful missionary to follow, look no further than your own Book of Mormon. All the sons of Mosiah were legendary missionaries, but when I was a kid, my favorite was Ammon. The story of Ammon has a certain "Indiana Jones" flavor that makes it exciting. He's a master of the sling, he disarms his enemies (so to speak), and he talks boldly to kings. I imagined him with biceps as big as those of any NFL star in my stack of football cards. As I grew up a little, however, I discovered a wealth of successful missionary principles hidden within Ammon's adventure. Let's identify them, shall we? Open your scriptures to Alma 17, and we'll go through it together.

First of all, Ammon went into the land of Ishmael to teach the Lamanites. Ammon was taken, bound, and brought before King Lamoni, and yet it seemed that Ammon knew exactly what he was doing. The king asked Ammon if he wanted to dwell among his people, and Ammon answered, "Yea, I desire to dwell among this people for a time; yea, and perhaps until the day I die" (Alma 17:23). The king was impressed with Ammon and ordered the servants to loosen his bands. Then Lamoni paid Ammon a supreme compliment by asking him, "Would you like to marry one of my daughters?" (If some girl's dad ever asks you that, trust me—it's a compliment.) Ammon responded beautifully—and you can only imagine what was going on in his head: *Marry one of his daughters? Hmmm, I guess maybe the mission president would frown on that*—anyway, Ammon's classic response was, "Nay, but I will be thy servant" (Alma 17:25).

And that, my future missionary friend, is the first principle: "*I will be thy servant.*" You know the missionary anthem, don't you? It begins, "Called to . . . " what? *Serve!* Notice that the song does not say, "Called to *prove* that you're wrong and I'm right, get a clue, bud, you're in the wrong church." Rather, it says, "Called to *serve*"! Why do you think missionaries do weekly service projects, hmmm? Serving others opens hearts and breaks down barriers. When people know that our motive is to serve and help them, it can have miraculous effects. If, on the other hand, we are going out to *prove* or contend, it makes people want to avoid us and invites a spirit of contention.

Okay, back to the story. Notice that Ammon still hadn't revealed that he was a missionary, at least not yet. What do you think the king was thinking at this point? Here comes this Nephite, he's tied up before the king, and he says, "Hi! I'm not from these parts, and I know you don't like Nephites, but I just want to live here perhaps until the day I die and be your slave! Can I, can I, can I?" The king responded, "Well, uh, sure, uh, we've been having some trouble with our sheep; maybe you could be a shepherd and tend my flocks." Did he ask Ammon to watch the flocks because he couldn't think of anything else for him to do? Perhaps not. Some have speculated that King Lamoni wanted to test Ammon's loyalty, to see if he really came to serve or if he had some other motive. That's a good point. If "called to serve" is just a catchy slogan or a nice song lyric, it isn't worth much. It's got to be real. You must develop a real love for people, especially the people among whom you will serve. When your motive is pure, you will want to serve them without expecting a reward, because you serve out of love.

Ammon watched the flocks with the other servants for three days before trouble came. As they were driving their flocks to the waters of Sebus, "a certain number of Lamanites . . . stood and scattered the flocks of Ammon and the servants of the king . . . insomuch that they fled many ways." The servants began to "weep exceedingly," because losing their flocks was a serious threat to their job security. The last time this happened, the servants were put to death! Ammon's reaction was completely opposite: "Now when Ammon saw this his heart was swollen within him for joy." Was Ammon rejoicing at someone else's problem? Not at all. He saw this as an opportunity to serve. "I will show forth my power unto these my fellow-servants, or the power which is in me, in restoring these flocks unto the king, that I may win the hearts of these my fellow-servants, that I may lead them to believe in my words" (Alma 17:27–29). Two principles of missionary work stick out to me in that last verse.

IT'S NOT YOUR POWER, IT'S THE POWER WITHIN YOU!

First, notice that Ammon corrected himself: "I will show forth my power . . . or the power that is in me . . . " He corrected himself because it was not his power! It was not his biceps! We, by ourselves, are *not* powerful! As Ammon explained later:

> Yea, I know that I am nothing; as to my strength I am weak; therefore I will not boast of myself, but I will boast of my God, for *in his strength* I can do all things; yea, behold, many mighty miracles we have wrought in this land, for which we will praise *his* name forever. (Alma 26:12; emphasis added)

It's important for us, as we serve, to remember our dependence on the Lord. Without him we are nothing! And with him we can do all things. The "power that is in us" comes from the Lord, and being too proud about our own abilities makes us lose that power.

WIN SOME HEARTS

The second thing that strikes me is Ammon's phrase, "that I may win the hearts of these my fellow-servants." This is a wonderful principle. Much of missionary work involves serving and winning hearts. The account goes on to say that "these were the thoughts of Ammon, when he saw the afflictions of those whom he termed to be his brethren" (Alma 17:30). Ammon didn't see the Lamanites only as contacts or investigators; he knew in his heart that they were his *brethren*, brothers and sisters in the family of Heavenly Father. So, how do you win hearts?

Four hundred and fifty teenagers won some hearts in Tennessee last summer at an "Especially for Youth" camp at Austin Peay State College. At the beginning of the week, I spoke to the group about Ammon and about "winning some hearts." I explained, "When you leave this place on Friday, the people on this campus won't know your name. But they'll remember you are LDS. Let's win a few hearts this weekend, shall we? When you go through the line in the cafeteria, when you get new towels from the 'Dorm

Mom,' when you interact with anyone on campus, do something that very few teenagers at other camps have ever done. Smile and say thank you. Treat people with kindness and respect. Keep your dorm rooms clean, keep the halls free from litter, and respect the grounds outside. Be uncommonly classy teenagers, okay?"

These youth were wonderful. They didn't need my help. I stood with them in the cafeteria line, and I heard them talk to the servers.

"Would you like chicken or fish?" asked the cafeteria lady.

"What's your name?" the young lady answered.

"Keesha," responded the slightly confused server.

"Keesha, I love your braids," answered the young lady as she walked away with her chicken. "What's your name?" she asked the next server.

"Barbara," another slightly confused worker answered.

"Thanks for serving us today."

"You're welcome," Barbara responded, wondering what in the world was going on.

Think of it. Four hundred and fifty classy teenagers, three meals a day, for five days. At the end of the week, the cafeteria workers were saying, "We don't want the students to come back; we like y'all!" On Friday, we gave away seven copies of the Book of Mormon. We won some hearts! Some of those hearts we knew about, and there may have been others as university employees watched our little LDS group from afar. Perhaps your mission call will be to Tennessee, and maybe you'll knock on the door of someone who'll be willing to listen to your words because some other Latter-day Saint laid the groundwork and won that person's heart.

As a missionary, you can win hearts too. You can be kind, courteous, happy, and friendly—even if people don't want to let you in! Leave their porch with a smile, and wish them a good day. If you see a piece of litter on the lawn, pick it up and throw it away! Be gushing out all over with love and service. This is not a "technique" to get converts, but an attitude that you can turn into a way of life.

Back to our story. Ammon encouraged the weeping servants and persuaded them to find their flocks and return them to the waters of Sebus. They "rushed forth with much swiftness" and succeeded in returning the flock. But the sheep scatterers were back, and they stood ready to chase the flocks away again. Now note the courage of Ammon: "But Ammon said unto his brethren: Encircle the flocks round about that they flee not; and I go and contend with these men who do scatter our flocks." "Contend" is quite an understatement for what Ammon did. Why did he think he could take on this group? Because Ammon knew and believed in the promises of the Lord. "The Lord had promised Mosiah that he would deliver his sons [including Ammon] out of their hands" (Alma 17:32–35).

Similar promises have been made by the Lord to you: "And whoso receiveth you, there I will be also, for I will go before your face. I will be on your right hand and on your left, and my Spirit shall be in your hearts, and mine angels round about you, to bear you up" (D&C 84:88).

Ammon, noting the lack of local law enforcement, began to "cast stones at them with his sling." The robbers, of course, threw stones right back at Ammon, but they were all air balls. So the men came after Ammon with clubs. Big mistake. "But behold, every man that lifted his club to smite Ammon, he smote off their arms with his sword; for he did withstand their blows by smiting their arms with the edge of his sword [okay, here comes the understatement of all time], insomuch that they began to be astonished . . . " When I first read this I thought to myself, "They *began* to be astonished? You cut off their arms and they're just *beginning* to be astonished? What would it take to really astonish these guys?" Okay, listen to the rest of the verse: "and [they] began to flee before him; yea, and they were not few in number; and he caused them to flee by the strength of his arm" (Alma 17:37).

What caused them to flee? *The strength of Ammon's arm.* Wait a minute. Didn't I just say that Ammon's success was a result not of his power, but of the power that was *in* him? Yes, I did. You see, when you're doing the Lord's work, it's not . . . well, I'll explain using another scripture: "And *their* arm shall be *my* arm, and I will be their shield and their buckler; and I will gird up their loins, and they shall fight manfully for me; and their enemies shall be under their feet; and I will let fall the sword in their behalf, and by the fire of mine indignation will I preserve them" (D&C 35:14; emphasis added). Once again, Ammon had courage because he knew whose work he was doing, and it can be the same for you. It's the Lord's work, your arm is his arm, and he is your ally. You don't need to fear.

Now, after Ammon had driven away the marauders, you can just imagine the conversation among the Lamanite servants:

"That was incredible!"

"Yeah, let's go tell the king."

"He won't believe us."

"Yes he will—pick up those arms!" So they took the arms in to the king (yuck!) and told him the whole story. The king listened intently and began to wonder. Until this moment, King Lamoni had supposed that "whatsoever [he] did was right; nevertheless, Lamoni began to fear exceedingly, with fear lest he had done wrong in slaying his servants" (Alma 18:5).

What is happening here? Well, Moroni tells us that everyone—member, nonmember, active, less-active—has the light of Christ, or a conscience (see Moroni 7). Perhaps seeing Ammon's great deeds awakened the conscience of King Lamoni to the point where he began to feel he shouldn't have slain his former shepherds for letting the flocks be scattered. What could this mean for you as a modern missionary? Let me illustrate with another example: Although I never swore, I knew plenty of people at school who used a lot of foul language. But I always noticed that they would reduce their swearing when I was around. Why was that? Perhaps, although they might never outwardly acknowledge that swearing was wrong, they knew it inwardly. And being around someone who didn't swear awakened their consciences and made them rethink their actions.

What is the principle here? Paul teaches, "Let no man despise thy youth; but *be thou an example of the believers*, in word, in conversation, in charity, in spirit, in faith, in purity" (1 Timothy 4:12; emphasis added). People you meet who have had no previous contact with the Church will judge all nine million of its members by you. So "be thou an example of the believers"! Your example will awaken the conscience of others and prepare them to hear more of the truth.

Back to the action: King Lamoni, after listening to this amazing turn of events, guessed that Ammon might be the Great Spirit. The servants responded, "Whether he be the Great Spirit or a man, we know not . . . [but] we know he is a friend unto the king" (Alma 18:3). What a wonderful statement! Jesus was called the Good Shepherd because he was willing to "lay down his life for the sheep." Similarly, Ammon's loyalty, his willingness to lay down his life for the king's sheep, was evidence that his earlier statement, "I will be thy servant," wasn't just words; he really was a friend to the king. Do you want to be a fine missionary? Be a friend.

King Lamoni finally asked, "Where is this man that has such great power? And they said unto him: Behold, he is feeding thy horses." Now, as you can imagine, King Lamoni was beginning to be astonished too. "Surely there has not been any servant among all my servants that has been as faithful as this man; for even he doth remember all my commandments to execute them" (Alma 18:10). Ammon had made quite an impression on King Lamoni. He had distinguished himself not only as a faithful servant, but as the *most* faithful servant King Lamoni had ever had! How do you think that affected King Lamoni's attitude toward Ammon?

After Ammon finished preparing the horses, he came in to the king, perhaps to ask what else he could do. The record states that "the countenance of the king was changed" and Ammon was about to turn around and leave. One of the king's servants broke the silence and said, "Rabbanah, which is, being interpreted, powerful or great king, . . . the king desireth thee to stay." Ammon turned back, and with that "called to serve" attitude said, "What wilt thou that I should do for thee, O king? And the king answered him not *for the space of an hour . . .* " (Alma 18:14; emphasis added). Whoa. That's a long time. (Aren't you glad that part isn't on the video?) Ammon asked again, "What desireth thou of me?" And the king said nothing.

The Spirit of the Lord, which is promised to every faithful missionary, helped Ammon discern the thoughts of the king, and he asked, "Is it because thou hast heard that I defended thy servants and thy flocks, and slew seven of their brethren with the sling and with the sword, and smote off the arms of others, in order to defend thy flocks and thy servants; behold, is it this that causeth thy marvelings? I say unto you, what is it, that thy marvelings are so great? Behold, I am a man, and am thy servant; therefore, whatsoever thou desirest which is right, that will I do" (Alma 18:16–17).

Finally the king couldn't stand it anymore; he asked, "Art thou that Great Spirit, who knows all things? Ammon answered and said unto him: I am not." Then King Lamoni asked Ammon to explain his ability to discern thoughts and his power in defending the sheep. He offered to give Ammon anything he desired. The king was so blown away, he even offered to guard Ammon with his armies, but then concluded that Ammon was more powerful than his armies anyway. Now, here comes one of my favorite verses: "Now Ammon being wise, yet harmless, he said unto Lamoni: Wilt thou hearken unto my words, if I tell thee by what power I do these things? And this is the thing I desire of thee" (Alma 18:22).

What was the thing Ammon wanted most? To teach. The king would have given him anything he wanted, and what did he ask for? Two P-days a week? A tour of Ishmael National Park? A different daily schedule so he could sleep in? No. Ammon was not a slacker. He didn't go on a mission to mess around. Ammon went to serve. He wanted to lead people to God. All he wanted was for the king to listen. Another thing—I love the combination of adjectives used: "Ammon being wise, yet harmless." Wisdom alone will not get you into doors. But wisdom coupled with humility, meekness, kindness . . . that just might do it.

Ammon proceeded to teach King Lamoni about God, the creation of the world, the journey of Lehi and his sons, and the plan of salvation. The king believed all of Ammon's words, and he cried unto the Lord, "O Lord, have mercy." Notice that he didn't turn to Ammon for forgiveness. Apparently Ammon had made it clear that he was only a messenger of the truth, and that the king must turn to the Lord for forgiveness. It's a fascinating story, and it just keeps getting better, because eventually the king's wife and many others are converted. Ammon's love for King Lamoni impresses King Lamoni's father so much that eventually he is converted too!

Now, here's an interesting question. If Ammon had started lecturing the king and telling him about the false traditions of his fathers when he was first brought in as a prisoner, would it have had the same effect? Instead Ammon demonstrated loyalty, service, duty, and even a willingness to risk his life for the king's sheep. He "built a relationship of trust" (you'll hear that phrase again when you get to the MTC). His "called to serve" attitude changed everything. You've heard it before, and you'll hear it again, and it will always be true: "People don't care how much you know until they know how much you care."

As a missionary, you are engaged in a wonderful work, part of a historic and glorious legacy. You join the ranks of New Testament missionaries like Peter and Paul. You stand with Book of Mormon missionaries like Abinadi, Alma, Amulek, Ammon, and Aaron. You serve with Parley P. Pratt, Wilford Woodruff, and Matthew Cowley. Many of the principles of missionary work you will have to learn from your own experience, line upon line, precept upon precept. Much of the wisdom you will need, however, is found right there in your own scriptures. I strongly encourage you to read Alma 17–26, and read it with the heart of a prospective missionary. Pray to the Lord for inspiration, look for the principles of missionary work within the record, and ponder them deeply.

When you're out there going from house to house, knocking on doors and talking to people, keep a peaceful smile on your face and remember the first six words of your mission call: *"You are hereby called to serve."*

"I Must Obey"

Obedience is the first law of heaven. All progression, all perfection, all salvation, all godliness, all that is right and just and true, all good things come to those who live the laws of Him who is Eternal. There is nothing in all eternity more important than to keep the commandments of God. —Bruce R. McConkie[1]

I don't know exactly how to put this in my planner, but I have an appointment in the next life. The prophet Nephi, yes, *the* Nephi wants to meet me, and he wants to meet you too. At least that's what I understand from these verses: "I have charity for my people, and great faith in Christ that I shall meet many souls spotless at his judgment-seat . . . and you and I shall stand face to face" (2 Nephi 33:7, 11). I can hardly wait for that day! Imagine standing before Nephi and thinking: "Wow, you're Nephi! You're him. You slew Laban, you made a bow from wood, you saw the Lord, you crossed the desert, you built a ship!" Won't that be something? I don't think I'll know what to say. I feel that I came to know Nephi a little bit on my mission. He was the model of obedience. When Laman and Lemuel said, "It is a hard thing," Nephi said, "I will go." When the Lord said, "Thou shalt build a ship," Nephi said, "Whither shall I go that I may find ore?" He did everything he was asked. And because Nephi was obedient, the Lord made him unstoppable.

Nephi was asked by the Lord to do some very difficult things. But he responded with an attitude of "I will go," believing and trusting that the Lord would "prepare a way" (see 1 Nephi 3:7). The rules you will be asked to obey on your mission will probably not be as hard as traveling through a desert to retrieve plates of brass, or building a ship for your family to cross an ocean in. They may be as simple as getting up on time every day. Whatever your mission rules are, Nephi can help you understand the best attitude to have toward them. You've seen different attitudes toward rules all your life. Hopefully, you'll see only the best attitudes on your mission.

OBEDIENCE AND SPIRITUAL MATURITY

Your attitude toward the mission rules is a great indicator of your spiritual maturity. My mission president told me that there was a large percentage of missionaries that he never had to worry about. These elders and sisters were hardworking, self-motivated, and self-governing. He could leave them alone in an area, tell them to go to work, and never worry about them again. To them, obedience to mission rules was a quest, not an irritation.

A smaller percentage of missionaries needed some contact. They needed encouragement and some degree of supervision. They required more of the mission president's time. They were okay, as long as someone checked up on their progress from time to time. "Are you getting up on time? Are you working hard? Everything okay?" To them, obedience was a duty that they needed to be reminded about.

Unfortunately, there was sometimes another group: a few who needed almost constant supervision. The mission president spent much of his time on this group—much more than he wanted to. To them, the mission rules were just a bunch of statements designed to make their lives hard. Somehow, they hadn't caught the spirit of the work. Maybe they'd come around someday—I'm sure the president hoped so, anyway.

Now, let me take a stab here. My guess is, if you are reading my words right now, you belong to the *"obedience is a quest"* category. You are self-governing, you don't need any kind of external control, and you genuinely want to be a good missionary. Why else would you be sitting here reading a Church book? My guess is that no one is forcing you to read this. It was probably a gift from Mom or Dad, but you're reading it because you want to. And that scares me a little, because if valiant people like you are reading it, I want to make sure that it's full of good stuff. I want to make sure that it actually does help you become a better missionary. So, do you really want to be a better missionary? Want my advice? Well, then, at the risk of repeating myself, here it comes: *Obey the mission rules, and obey them because you want to.*

BROKEN LAWS OR BROKEN PEOPLE?

We use an interesting word to describe what happens when people don't keep the rules. We say they "broke" the law. But did the law break? Is it damaged in any way? Or did the *people* break?

"We can't really 'break' the law," someone once said, "we can only break ourselves against the law." It's true. You know from high school science class that every action brings a reaction, and every cause has an effect. If you jump off a building, the *law* of gravity says you will fall. Now, if we wanted to, we could write to our representatives in Congress and ask them to repeal the law of gravity, but the law would remain intact. Certain laws can't be changed.

Like the law of gravity, the Ten Commandments are laws we can't alter or repeal. They are eternal laws. Legislatures and parliaments can get together and pretend to change God's laws, but it has no effect on eternal truth. We only break ourselves when we go against the laws that cannot be changed.

So, rather than break ourselves against the laws, why don't we use the laws to help the Lord do his work? Here is an eternal law that you can use to your advantage. It will help you succeed as a missionary and throughout your life:

> There is a law, irrevocably decreed in heaven before the foundations of this world, upon which all blessings are predicated—And when we obtain any blessing from God, it is by obedience to that law upon which it is predicated. (D&C 130:20–21)

OBEDIENCE BRINGS BLESSINGS

It's a law, an irrevocable law, and it has been in force since before the world was created: blessings are a natural consequence of keeping the rules. It's a matter of action and reaction. One of the things you will teach people on your mission is that the commandments are guidelines to happiness. People who steal, covet, dishonor their parents, or lie on a regular basis *cannot* be happy. It's against the law!

As you reflect back on your own life, you will realize that you are happiest when you are keeping the commandments. You feel more faith, you feel a stronger testimony, you feel happier, and you love life. Alma stated it this way: "Wickedness never was happiness" (Alma 41:10).

Obedience certainly doesn't guarantee that you won't

have trials—you will. Many people who keep all the commandments seem to experience lots of trials. (Look at Abraham, Abinadi, Nephi, and Jesus!) But their obedience gives them something *better* than happiness—it's called *peace.* Peace comes when you know inside that you're doing your best. And when you're doing your best, the Lord makes up for the rest.

Obedience can't guarantee baptisms, either. People still have their agency. Nephi's brothers saw angels, and they still didn't change. You'll find on your mission that some people simply won't join the Church even when they've felt the Spirit. As the hymn says, "God will force no man to heaven" (*Hymns,* no. 240). We are obedient as missionaries, however, because we want to give ourselves every chance to succeed. Our job is to do all we can to qualify for the Spirit, and one of those things we can do is be obedient to mission rules.

Here's another eternal law, given by the Lord himself in the Doctrine and Covenants: "I, the Lord, am bound when ye do what I say; but when ye do not what I say, ye have no promise" (D&C 82:10). There were times on my mission when my companion and I would try to "bind" the Lord. That may sound strange, so let me explain: we would try to keep the mission rules with exactness, so that we could take advantage of the Lord's promise, "I, the Lord, am *bound* when ye do what I say." We would do everything in our power, then ask for the Lord to make up the difference.

It's much easier to ask the Lord for blessings when we're keeping the rules. How could we expect blessings if we weren't willing to be obedient? It would be like asking, "Please bless us as we rob this bank that we may return home in safety."

OBEDIENCE STRENGTHENS FAITH

As you are more obedient, you can expect more blessings, and eternal law says that they will come. In this way, *obedience strengthens faith*. Elder Bruce R. McConkie said: "Faith is a gift of God bestowed as a reward for personal righteousness. It is always given when righteousness is present, and the greater the measure of obedience to God's laws the greater will be the endowment of faith."[2] It's true: your faith increases as you keep the rules.

When you arrive at the MTC, they'll give you a small white *Missionary Handbook*. It's small enough for an elder to keep it in his shirt pocket behind his name tag. Over the years, many missionaries have referred to it as the "white bible." Inside are specific instructions about your calling, your conduct, your daily schedule, and many other mission rules. The *Missionary Handbook* is a book of rules, but it's more than that—it's like a mini success guide. Many times during my mission, as I was riding the bus or waiting in a line or something, I would read and reread my "white bible." This way I was sure I knew all the rules and was keeping them.

You might also have more rules that are specific to your mission. For example, the "white bible" says to arise at 6:30 A.M., but in our mission, it was 6:00 A.M. This made sense, because in the Philippines most people went to bed right after the sun went down, so we would compensate by getting up earlier and going to bed earlier. There may be specific changes in your mission too. There may be rules about your preparation day activities, the music you can listen to, and the food you eat (it was a mission rule in the Philippines to boil your water before you drank it). You may not understand all the reasons behind some of the rules. Obey them anyway—not out of blindness, but out of faith.

BLIND OBEDIENCE VERSUS FAITH OBEDIENCE

If you were to ask a member of the Church back in 1835 why he didn't use tobacco, what would he say? "Well, uh, it's because of an addictive chemical called nicotine that acts as a stimulant, increases the heart rate, and can lead to lung cancer, emphysema, and heart disease." Did anyone know about those things back in 1835? No. In fact, even in the 1940s, a hundred years later, they still didn't know. They actually advertised that cigarette smoking "aided digestion." Today there is ample medical evidence to validate the Word of Wisdom, but in 1835 the Saints could only respond by saying, "The Lord has asked us not to." If you don't understand some of the mission rules, have the faith to obey even though you don't know why.

When an angel asked Adam why he offered sacrifices, Adam said, "I know not, save the Lord commanded me." Then the angel told Adam the reason (see Moses 5:6–8). Notice the sequence: Adam obeyed first; then the angel told him why. Perhaps, during the course of your mission, you'll learn the reasons behind all the mission rules. Perhaps you won't. Joseph Smith taught, "Whatever God requires is right, no matter what it is, although we may not see the reason thereof until long after the events transpire."[3]

The best missionaries are more interested in keeping the rules than in knowing all the reasons for them. This is not blind obedience, but faith obedience. We exercise faith in the Lord, in the mission president, and in the eternal laws of obedience, and we keep *all* the rules—not just the ones we fully understand. Elder Boyd K. Packer stated it beautifully: "Those who talk of blind obedience may appear to know many things, but they do not understand the doctrines of the gospel. There is an obedience that comes from a knowledge of the truth that transcends any external form of control. We are not obedient because we are blind, we are obedient because we can see."[4]

OBEDIENCE HELPS YOU RADIATE YOUR MESSAGE

Sister missionaries served in a part of my mission called the "refugee camp." I visited there once, and it changed my life. Refugees from Laos, Cambodia, and other oppressed countries fled to the Philippines, where numerous international charitable organizations helped prepare them for life in the United States. The sisters had some very difficult mission rules to follow: don't teach the gospel; don't baptize; just give Christian service and prepare these people for life in the states. The sisters taught the refugees English phrases, the names of the months, the holidays, and the days of the week, but they couldn't say a word about the gospel. The rules of the United Nations forbade it. Some other religious organizations disobeyed the rules, but we wouldn't.

Does obedience really bring blessings? Wouldn't it be blessing these people to teach them the gospel, even if it broke a little rule? Nope. Remember, *eternal laws have consequences.*

A year or so after I returned from the Philippines, Elder Marion D. Hanks gave a talk about the refugee camp. He said:

> I know a young lady and her companions who served helping refugees in Asia, never able to teach a formal religious discussion because they were honest in keeping camp rules, even though others sometimes did not. After a time, a man who had been very unsympathetic to any Mormon helping in the refugee camps, because he thought we were not really interested in anything but aggressive proselyting, wrote a letter, a letter of apology and commendation. I will

read a sentence or two: "There is still a great deal of fear among other voluntary agencies that the Mormons are here to proselyte. Even if you don't talk about your religion, your values come across like a ton of bricks and that frightens people. You live what you believe. Therein may lie your problem—especially when it brings such inner strength, peace, and confidence as you girls radiate."[5]

A person who is obedient radiates. Such a person's values "come across like a ton of bricks." Although the sister missionaries didn't proselyte, they had an impact. The refugees often wrote letters back to the sisters, telling incredible stories of how they found the Church once they arrived in the states. One might see a pair of young men in his new town who were wearing black name tags, just like the sisters. Another would recognize the name of the Church on a building, remember the spirit the sisters radiated, and begin to take the discussions. Many were baptized in the United States by other missionaries. But the amazing thing is this: the sister missionaries in the refugee camps planted the seeds of the gospel *without saying a word!* President David O. McKay taught:

> Every man and every person who lives in this world wields an influence, whether for good or for evil. It is not what he says alone; it is not alone what he does. It is what he is. Every man, every person radiates what he or she really is . . . . It is what we are and what we radiate that affects the people around us.[6]

If sisters in the refugee camp could bring people into the Church without saying a word, imagine what you could do if, in addition to the radiance of your obedience, you could share your feelings and your testimony!

So, let's review: What are some of the eternal laws about obedience?

1. *Obedience brings blessings.*
2. *Obedience strengthens faith.*
3. *Obedience helps you radiate your message.*

I'd like to add one more: *Obedience brings freedom.* It's a curious concept, but it's true. Think about it. You know it's true from your own life. Those who study hard in high school have the freedom to choose from among many colleges which one they will attend. Those who choose to mess around instead of study will have to search for a college that will take them. Those who have kept the Word of Wisdom are free to enjoy physical health and peace of conscience, while those who "broke" the rules, addicting themselves to drugs and alcohol, are now enjoying their "freedom" behind bars or in rehab centers. Elder Boyd K. Packer taught:

> Obedience—that which God will never take by force—He will accept when freely given. And He will then return to you freedom that you can hardly dream of—the freedom to feel and to know, the freedom to do, and the freedom to *be*, at least a thousandfold more than we offer Him. Strangely enough, the key to freedom is obedience.[7]

Keep the mission rules, follow the counsel of your mission president, put your agency in the Lord's hands, and He'll be free to make you the best missionary you can possibly be.

SOME CAUTIONS

Anyone who reads this chapter may think of some exceptions to the rules. Of course, there will be times when you have to choose between conflicting good things. Welcome to reality. This is when you'll have to use your head, your heart, and your inspiration. For example, in our mission, it was a rule to drink fluids when fasting. This rule was necessary to keep missionaries from dehydrating in the tropical heat. It was an exception to the usual rules about fasting—and sometimes in life these exceptions crop up.

But this chapter is not about exceptions. If you want to be truly at peace, don't be one of those missionaries who seem to be constantly searching for a way around the rules. Remember, "The Lord requireth the heart and a willing mind; and the willing and obedient shall eat the good of the land of Zion in these last days" (D&C 64:34). A "willing mind" is not one that is always looking for exceptions to the rules.

Another caution: you need to be careful not to offend others in your quest to be obedient. Sometimes on my mission, in order to make sure our members and investigators didn't think we were being purposely rude, we would have to explain our rules. "I'm sorry, but we have to get home. It's one of our mission rules to be in by 9:30, and we always want to show the Lord our willingness to keep his commandments and obey the mission rules." Members and investigators are very supportive of missionaries who are trying their best to do things right. When you explain things carefully, they'll understand.

Great blessings are available to you on your mission, and you largely determine whether you'll receive them or not. Elder Robert D. Hales taught:

> Unless missionaries choose obedience, consecrating all of their time, talents and resources in the service of the Lord while they are in the mission field, they cannot fully realize all the great blessings the Lord has in store for them.[8]

I feel inadequate to express how important it is to keep

the mission rules throughout your mission. There is a direct correlation between obedience and peace. You'll see! The world is already full of slackers and whiners. The Lord doesn't need any more in the mission field. Let Nephi be your example. Whatever the Lord asked, Nephi did it. He repeatedly did what seemed impossible. He did it even when he didn't know how he was going to do it. He did it while enduring the constant murmuring of his brothers. He moved his whole family along when his parents were too weak to help. He did it because he was deeply committed to God. He obeyed because he wanted to. His final testimony was a plea for all of us to come unto Christ. To me, the last three words Nephi wrote reveal how he felt about obedience. Make them your missionary motto, too: "I must obey."

---

1. Bruce R. McConkie, *The Promised Messiah* (Salt Lake City: Deseret Book, 1981), p. 126.
2. Bruce R. McConkie, *Mormon Doctrine*, s.v. "Faith" (Salt Lake City: Bookcraft, 1979), p. 264.
3. *Teachings of the Prophet Joseph Smith*, comp. Joseph Fielding Smith (Salt Lake City: Deseret Book, 1976), p. 256.
4. *Ensign*, May 1983, p. 66.
5. In *Brigham Young University Speeches of the Year*, 1985–86, pp. 3–4.
6. David O. McKay, *Man May Know For Himself*, compiled by Clare Middlemiss (Salt Lake City: Deseret Book, 1967), p. 108.
7. Boyd K. Packer, *That All May Be Edified* (Salt Lake City: Bookcraft, 1988), p. 256.
8. *Ensign*, May 1990, p. 41.

PART THREE
The Lord,
My Companion,
and Me

When the Spirit is present, people are not offended when you share your feelings about the gospel.

—M. Russell Ballard

The Spirit Converts

*I will go before your face. I will be on your right
hand and on your left, and my Spirit shall be
in your hearts, and mine angels round about
you, to bear you up.* —D&C 84:88

As you walk down the street with your companion, it
appears to most of the world that there are only two of
you. In reality, there are three. Never forget this most
important trio: "The Lord, my companion, and me." It is
this trio that does missionary work. Without the Lord, you
just do a whole lot of walking for two years. Without your
companion, you lose power, protection, and the promise
of the Holy Ghost. And without you, *all* of you, your
whole heart and soul, the Lord lacks an instrument
through which he can do his work.

You take the Lord's name upon you in a spiritual way
every time you take the sacrament, but on a mission you
do it physically. It's no small thing to have the name "Jesus
Christ" attached to your suit or your dress. You'll want to
watch what you do, because you represent him now. As
you may remember from earlier in the book, one of the

main things I wondered after I opened my call was what kind of shirts I would wear. I am so embarrassed. What a stupid thing to be thinking about! I guess I was still in high school mode, overly concerned about my clothes. When I got into the mission field, I put away the high school things, and started to grow up (see 1 Corinthians 13:11). The most important part of my wardrobe then was a little badge that said, "Elder Bytheway—The Church of Jesus Christ of Latter-day Saints." Inside my "white bible" was a small, certificate-type thing. It was my I.D. Underscored by President Spencer W. Kimball's signature, it certified that I was "a duly ordained minister of the gospel." I remember reading those words for the first time and thinking, *Me? An ordained minister? No way.*

We talked about Ammon in the chapter titled "Called to Serve." Now I'd like to add one more word: "Called to Serve *Him.*" Remember who you're serving and why you're out there. What a relief it is to have such a powerful third member in your companionship! You don't have to serve alone.

I love the Lord. He helped me so much on my mission. He helped me know what to say. He watched over me. At times, he seemed to pick me up and carry me home.

One night Elder Lewis and I were walking back to our apartment. I was so discouraged. We had been teaching a wonderful, humble man. He was an older man, a kind and soft-spoken Lutheran deacon. When we went back for the third discussion, he answered the door and told us that he didn't want us to come back anymore. I was very disappointed. As I walked, I remember thinking, *I wish I were President Thomas S. Monson, I wish I were Elder Neal A. Maxwell—maybe then I would've known the words to say to convince him to listen to us again. Maybe then he would've felt the Spirit and joined the Church. I just can't do this right—I'm too young, too inexperienced . . .*

At that moment, a thought came into my mind with great impact. Actually, it was a thought mixed with a scripture: *Elder, you don't have to be President Monson or Elder Maxwell. All you have to do is have the Holy Ghost. Then what you say will be the will of the Lord, the mind of the Lord, and the voice of the Lord. Elder Bytheway, the Spirit converts.*

I didn't know the reference, but I knew I had seen those words before. At our apartment, I scoured my scriptures until I found the verse that had come into my mind. The words weren't exactly the same, but I know this is the verse the Lord helped me remember:

> And whatsoever they shall speak when moved upon by the Holy Ghost shall be scripture, shall be the will of the Lord, shall be the mind of the Lord, shall be the word of the Lord, shall be the voice of the Lord, and the power of God unto salvation.
>
> Behold, this is the promise of the Lord unto you, O ye my servants.
>
> Wherefore, be of good cheer, and do not fear, for I the Lord am with you, and will stand by you; and ye shall bear record of me, even Jesus Christ, that I am the Son of the living God, that I was, that I am, and that I am to come. (D&C 68:4–6)

As I read those words, I felt as though the Lord was talking to me. And he was talking to me so tenderly. "Be of good cheer, and do not fear, for I the Lord am with you, and will stand by you." This initial disappointment became one of my most remembered spiritual experiences. *This isn't my work,* I remember thinking. *It is the Lord's work, and he will help me!* I also resolved that I would do better, that I would work harder, that I would make sure I was worthy to have the Holy Ghost with me at all times.

Several weeks later, I was in the same area with a new companion. An investigator gave us the name of a seventy-five-year-old man. He was an engineer, an educated man, and he was very down on religion. When we showed up on his porch, he looked us up and down and said, "You're very young. I doubt you can teach me anything." I knew *I* couldn't teach him much, but I also knew that the Holy Ghost could teach him everything. He agreed to listen to us the next day, and we prepared to teach him about Joseph Smith's First Vision.

Elder Warren began to teach, and we noticed that our investigator was rather anxious and fidgety. He'd look at the floor, then at the ceiling, then off to the side. It was as if he was trying to avoid eye contact, and I don't think he heard a word of what we were saying.

After a few moments, he interrupted me in midsentence as he almost yelled, *"Who created evil?"* We all sat silent. In all my years of Sunday School, seminary, and priesthood meetings, I had never heard that question before. I believe our third companion began to help us at this point. Suddenly, in my mind, I understood his real question: Did *God* create evil? If he did, how could he be God?

I picked up my Bible and said, "Sir, it has to do with a place called the premortal existence," and I began to explain. From the look on his face, I could tell he'd never heard anything like this before. I referred to the book of Isaiah, and told him about Lucifer, the son of the morning, who by his own choice rebelled against God and fell from heaven, becoming the father of lies and the father of evil.

He remained silent for a second, then nodded slowly as if to say, "Okay—I'll buy that for now . . . " I felt relieved that he was satisfied with our response, so we tried to continue where we left off. But Brother Sajonas stopped us again at midsentence and loudly demanded, *"Why are there so many wars?"*

At this point I was glad I had listened in U.S. History class. Looking into those intense, seventy-five-year-old eyes, I knew that he had witnessed much of World War II. I knew that the Japanese had invaded the Philippines, and that his country was later retaken by U.S. forces. He must have seen a lot of horrible things that would bring anyone to question the existence of God.

Fortunately, the answer came again. "You see, sir, it has to do with something we possessed in the premortal existence. It's called agency." I explained how people have a hard time getting along with one another, and that this is true about leaders of nations as well. Sometimes we don't do a very good job of running this world, and we get in fights and in wars. God doesn't want the wars, and he is often pained by our actions, but part of the plan is that he leaves us free to choose between evil and good. If God came down and solved all our problems, we wouldn't be able to learn and grow from our own experience, and that's what life is for.

This answer seemed to get him thinking, and we continued with our discussion. He waited a minute and then stopped us a third time and asked, *"Why do so many children starve?"* That was a good question! Elder Warren and I had seen things in the Philippines that we'd never seen in Utah. Malnutrition and poverty were almost everywhere we looked. Little children, really little, some not even old enough to walk, would crawl and play around the open sewers. Many had no clothes. Some would get parasites that stunted their growth. Others had patchy rashes on their heads that would cause their hair to fall out. Some had open cuts and wounds that weren't properly cleaned and bandaged and never seemed to heal. I had asked

myself the same question. I tried to explain it to Brother
Sajonas. "Heavenly Father has a different perspective than
we do. When we see a child die, that's how we see it: a
child dying. Heavenly Father, on the other hand, sees one
of his own spirit children being set free and coming home
to him after being away for only a very short time." At this
point, it dawned on us that we were teaching the wrong
lesson. The answers to each of his questions were integral
parts of the plan of salvation. We should have been teaching the Purpose of Life discussion!

The introductory visual aid for that discussion listed
three questions. I turned to it and began to explain. A
change of expression came over his face, and I watched
him in silence as he read and reread each question.

Where did I come from?

Why am I here?

Where am I going after this life?

His eyes moistened, and tears fell from his face. I had
never had this reaction with this picture or any other in my
flip chart, and I wasn't sure what was going on. I looked at
Elder Warren, and back at Brother Sajonas. Just then, our
third companion spoke words to my mind: "Elder . . .
Testify." (It has always been interesting to me that the
Spirit would use my priesthood title.) I knew it was time
to bear my testimony. I sat up on the edge of the bench,
looked in Brother Sajonas's eyes, and with the boldness of
all my nineteen years testified to him that we knew where
we came from, why we were here, and where we were
going. I told him that we were representatives of the Lord's
church, and that we were sent to teach him these things.
He didn't speak. He pushed himself up, motioned for us
to wait, and walked slowly to the back of the room.
Retrieving a little red book from a shelf, he made his way
back to where we were sitting. He opened the book to the

back, held it up in front of my face, and said tearfully, "You are so young!" I saw that he had written some things on the back inside cover. In an old man's shaky handwriting, it said:

My Eternal Questions
1. Where did I come from?
2. Why am I here?
3. What do I need to accomplish?
4. Where will I go when I die?

After I read the words, I looked back up into this sweet old man's teary eyes as he said, "You are so young. And you've come from so far to teach me these things." The next day we displayed the entire plan of salvation on his table with little cardboard visual aids. We had a wonderful discussion. In the middle of the lesson, I remember watching Brother Sajonas bow his head, cover his face with his hands, and sob, "I have been looking for this for forty years." What an experience! We weren't President Monson and Elder Maxwell, but it didn't matter, because the Lord sent the Holy Ghost. And the Holy Ghost can work with young missionaries—even Elder Warren and Elder Bytheway. The promises of the Doctrine and Covenants are true!

> Therefore, verily I say unto you, lift up your voices unto this people; speak the thoughts that I shall put into your hearts, and you shall not be confounded before men;
>
> For it shall be given you in the very hour, yea, in the very moment, what ye shall say.
>
> But a commandment I give unto you, that ye shall declare whatsoever thing ye declare in my name, in solemnity of heart, in the spirit of meekness, in all things.
>
> And I give unto you this promise, that inasmuch as

ye do this the Holy Ghost shall be shed forth in bearing record unto all things whatsoever ye shall say. (D&C 100:5–8)

Sometimes missionaries misunderstand. At times, they might think that enthusiasm brings conversion. *If I'm just really excited in my teaching, they'll see that the gospel makes me happy, and they'll want to join the Church too.* At other times, they might think that logic brings conversion. *If I can show them all the scriptures, and I'm really good at showing them why our church is right, then I'm sure I can convince them that we have the truth.* Or they may believe that friendship brings conversion. *We'll just be buds with them, and hang out with them, and then they'll want to join.* Each of these things may be helpful to some degree, and each of them may "win hearts" and eventually give you an opportunity to teach. But none of them brings lasting *conversion.* The Lord must be involved. All of my experiences as a missionary reinforced a truth that I had heard all my life. I just had to gain a testimony of it on a deeper level. That truth is: *The Spirit converts.*

I loved it when investigators would say, "Whenever you elders come over, there's such a different feeling here. And it seems that when you leave, the feeling leaves too." We heard that often, and we always responded, "That feeling is the Holy Ghost, and he's telling you that the things we're teaching are good, and right, and true. Would you like to have that feeling all the time? It's called the gift of the Holy Ghost . . . "

When I learned this important principle, that the Spirit converts, I made it my main goal to be worthy so that the Spirit could accompany our teaching. When we were finished with a discussion, we would close with prayer and quickly excuse ourselves. If we stayed too long, and mingled and joked around, the Spirit would slowly leave. I wanted the Spirit to leave at the same time we did, so our investigators would notice the sudden contrast.

I know I still have a lot to learn about how the Spirit works, and you will learn new things daily on your mission. Remember that the Lord and his Spirit are on your side. And if you ever start feeling weighed down by the pressures of missionary work, open your eyes and take a good look at your name badge. Remember, in a way, your mission isn't really yours. It is the Lord's work, and you are his servant. You carry his name on your lapel, and you want to be sure you also carry it in your heart. He wants people to be taught and baptized even more than you do! He is eager to send his Spirit to testify of the truth of what you are teaching. So be obedient and purify your heart and motives so that the Holy Ghost can accompany you. In every thought, look to the Lord, the most important member of your companionship. We are called to serve *him*, and without him, we are nothing (see John 15:15; Moses 1:10).

Being Different Together

And ye shall go forth in the power of my Spirit,
preaching my gospel, two by two, in my
name, lifting up your voices as with the sound
of a trump, declaring my word like unto
angels of God. —D&C 42:6

Missionary work is difficult. Imagine how hard it would be if you had to do it alone! Many missionaries in the early days of the Church were alone, but you will have a companion. What a blessing this is! You can talk to each other, encourage each other, and help each other. You eat together, pray together, and teach together.

Doctrine and Covenants 42:6 gives us high expectations—to speak "like angels of God." In order to be able to do that, we must do all we can to have the Spirit in our companionship. It will require some effort, but it's also kind of fun.

It's very mind-expanding to spend twenty-four hours a day with someone other than a member of your own family. It helps you to understand that we all see things through the lens of our own experience. Chances are, all your life you've hung out with people who are like you:

same likes, same dislikes, same values. Now you get a chance to spend time with someone who is, perhaps, much different from you.

I learned so much from my Filipino companions. Some came from very humble circumstances, but their testimonies were powerful and refined. No one who heard us teach together would say we were the same. But sameness is not the goal—the goal is brotherly kindness and harmony, and that brings the companionship of the Holy Ghost. As someone once said, "Harmony is the result of being different, together." And we were different, but we were together with our witness of the truth.

What makes a great companionship? Well, it comes down to the basics. One of my business classes at BYU required me to subscribe to the *Wall Street Journal*. One day, while perusing the paper, I noticed an interesting list:

Five Inadequacies that Contribute to the Failure of a Manager:[1]
1. Unable to get along with others
2. Unable to adapt to change
3. Suffer from the "me only" syndrome
4. Unwilling to put self on the line
5. Unable to rebound from a setback

It intrigued me that there was no mention of where a manager earned a business degree, or what grades he or she got. No mention of intelligence or aptitude. The number-one item on the list wasn't a business skill at all, it was a people skill—getting along with others.

I believe we could call the above list "Five Inadequacies that Contribute to the Failure of a *Missionary*." The ability to get along with others will affect you in virtually all areas of your life—your career, your marriage, and of course, your mission. You will have companions of all kinds on your mission; how well you get along with them will make a huge difference in how effective you are. Most important, you can't have the power of the Spirit with you if there are hard feelings in your companionship. On the other hand, if your relationship as companions is good, you'll be much more likely to have the Holy Ghost with you, and you'll have a wonderful time.

I'm not an expert on listening skills, counseling methods, or communication techniques, but I honestly believe you don't have to be in order to have a great companionship. You simply have to be Christlike. If you are Christlike, it means you are meek, humble, and teachable, and you can listen to honest criticism without taking offense. If you are Christlike, you are able to be patient, loving, and long-suffering.

Whenever I had a rough spot in my companionships, it usually came down to my own pride. When I was willing to admit this to myself, my problem was half solved. When my stake president, George I. Cannon, set me apart as a missionary, he challenged me to memorize Doctrine and Covenants section four and to repeat it to myself every day. Listen to the companionship counsel given in this great missionary scripture.

> For behold the field is white already to harvest; and lo, he that thrusteth in his sickle with his might, the same layeth up in store that he perisheth not, but bringeth salvation to his soul;
>
> And faith, hope, charity and love, with an eye single to the glory of God, qualify him for the work.
>
> Remember faith, virtue, knowledge, temperance, patience, brotherly kindness, godliness, charity, humility, diligence.
>
> Ask, and ye shall receive; knock, and it shall be opened unto you. Amen. (D&C 4:4–7)

What a great list of reminders of how to get along with

your companions! (Notice it doesn't say, "Remember listening skills, communication techniques . . . ") If the Lord is going to be part of your companionship, you must live by his rules.

It is said that the formula for reducing stress is found in two simple steps: "Step One: Don't sweat the small stuff. Step Two: Remember, it's all small stuff." I dare say that most of the little bumps in a companionship would be easily solved if we could stop looking at the "small stuff" and regain our perspective. Jesus was incredibly focused on the grand purpose at all times. He was always "about his Father's business" (see Luke 2:49). At times you may need to remind yourself about the "marvelous work and a wonder" of which you are a part, and forget that your companion squeezes the toothpaste in the wrong place or snores like a horse. (See, you just smiled, didn't you? And you can smile and insert earplugs on your mission too.)

Yes, there may be times when you have to talk to your companion about difficulties in your relationship. Just remember to exercise patience, brotherly kindness, charity, humility—in short, be Christlike!

Wrong: "Man, Elder Jones, would you stop chewing with your mouth open? You make me sick! With all that cereal in there sloshing around, you sound like a rock crusher."

Better: "Elder, when we have companionship inventory tonight, could I talk to you about something?" (Later): "Elder, you know I think you're a great elder, and I enjoy working with you. I admire you for the things you teach me. That door approach you did today was fantastic. There's just something that if you could help me with, I think it would make a difference in our companionship, and would make things easier for me. Would you mind if I told you about it? I know this is just a little thing, but I

guess that when I was growing up, I got used to certain eat-
ing habits, like chewing with my mouth closed, and I was
wondering if you'd consider doing that. It's not a big deal,
but I know it would help me. I just want us to have a great
companionship. Now, while we're on the subject, is there
anything that I do that gets on your nerves?"

I'm not trying to put words in your mouth, or tell you
how you should approach your companion problems, but
just to demonstrate the spirit of an effective problem-
solving discussion. Did you notice the mood of that example? It's not mean-spirited or accusing, but direct, honest, and clear. The spirit of meekness is its main
characteristic.

Being meek also means being able to accept criticism
without taking offense. If your companion has something
to say to you, consider it honestly. By accepting suggestions
and trying to improve, you will reap two benefits. First, you
will stop the behavior that annoys your companion.
Second, your companion will notice your honest effort in
his or her behalf, and this sacrifice will bring a greater
measure of the Spirit into your companionship.

One of my favorite examples of meekness comes from
the book of Alma, chapters 60 and 61. Captain Moroni,
leader of the Nephite army, sends a letter to Pahoran, the
governor of the land, mistakenly accusing him of sitting
on his throne in a "thoughtless stupor" while Moroni and
his army are suffering for lack of provisions. Moroni even
hints that Pahoran may be a traitor! Here is Pahoran's
Christlike response:

> And now, in your epistle you have censured me,
> but it mattereth not; I am not angry, but do rejoice in
> the greatness of your heart. I, Pahoran, do not seek for
> power, save only to retain my judgment-seat that I
> may preserve the rights and the liberty of my people.

My soul standeth fast in that liberty in the which God hath made us free. (Alma 61:9)

Not only does Pahoran refuse to take offense, but he acknowledges that Moroni has a great heart. He seems to recognize a great truth: that he and Moroni are both on the same side—the Lord's side. So are you and your companion.

Involve the Lord in finding solutions to your companionship problems, and you will be fine. This doesn't mean it will always be easy. No doubt, you will have some companions who are harder to love than others. I was lucky enough to have as one of my companions a friend of mine from high school. Elder Andrew and I had some great times. With some others, well, I had to make more of an effort.

Jesus taught: "For if ye love them which love you, what reward have ye? do not even the publicans the same? And if ye salute your brethren only, what do ye more than others? do not even the publicans so?" The next verse says it all: "Be ye therefore perfect, even as your Father which is in heaven is perfect" (Matthew 5:46–48). Perhaps part of being perfect is learning to love those who are hard to love. With some of my companions, just about the only thing we had in common was our membership in the Church. But what a great place to start! I became close friends with many of them.

Strive to forget yourself and serve. Learning to get along with your companion will help you later in life. President Spencer W. Kimball commented:

> If you can't get along with your companion, how can you get along with the person you choose to live with for the rest of your life? For your own sake, you must fit into your companion's life and adjust. Perhaps your homes are different. Grit your teeth and

say, "I am going to give about 90 percent and I will only take 10 percent." You have to "give and take" in every phase of life. How are you going to get along with a wife or husband? Just exactly the same way, a life of unselfishness and consideration for others. You must think of the other, love him more than your own self, and then you will have success.[2]

Sometimes the problems between companions are not "small stuff." You may run into trials more difficult to resolve than a simple toothpaste dispensing disagreement. Work through them prayerfully and meekly. If a problem becomes very serious, you may have to let your mission president know in your weekly letter to him. Take care of it, and don't let it affect the work.

You may have the blessing of having some incredible companions. Be grateful. Every single companion I had taught me something valuable. I learned things from brand-new missionaries and almost-home missionaries alike. It's so much fun when you get new companions to watch how they "intro" people, or how they do door approaches. President Ezra Taft Benson taught: "When you reach the point where you can enjoy and rejoice in the success of your companion, even when that success exceeds your own, then you have got real missionary spirit, the real unselfish spirit of love, the spirit of the gospel. When you can rejoice in the success of your companion, then you have a spirit that will make you effective as a missionary. Then you will really be truly, truly, happy."[3]

When I was four months out, I got a new companion who had been out twenty-one months. We learned a lot about the power of our good companionship from investigators and people on the street. We gradually came to realize that they were impressed by how we treated each other, how happy we were, and how fast we walked. On several occasions people asked Elder Steve Lewis and me, "Are you guys brothers? You seem so happy." What a perfect opportunity for us to tell them the *real* source of our happiness. Someone else asked us, "Why are you always walking so fast? Where are you going?" Another opportunity for a great answer: "Well, something wonderful has happened, and not many people know about it, and we're telling people about it as fast as we can." Then we would add with a smile, "If you want to make an appointment, we'd love to tell your family too." From then on, we made it a point to walk fast. It makes people wonder what's so urgent when they see you out there lengthening your stride and quickening your pace.

It's important that the impression we give matches our message. For example, would you buy an energy pill from a salesman who kept falling asleep during his presentation? Of course not. The message of the Restoration is amazing, fantastic, exciting! Think of what we are telling people. We're going all over the world proclaiming that God is once again speaking to prophets on the earth! If we come across as bored and detached, we're going to confuse a lot of investigators. This point is powerfully communicated by Elder Glenn L. Pace:

> In the mission field, my companion and I were teaching a Harvard University student. After we told him the Joseph Smith story and bore our testimonies to him, as we had done many times before, he said, "Wait a minute. Are you telling me you believe God and Christ appeared to Joseph Smith and told him he was to set up a new church?" We said we did believe that. He continued the interrogation: "You also believe an angel gave plates to Joseph Smith, who translated them into the Book of Mormon, and that the Savior appeared to the people on this continent?"

We said we did. "You also believe the president of your church is a prophet who receives revelation from God, as did Adam, Noah, and Abraham?" We said we did. Getting more animated by the minute, the investigator said, "That is the most incredible story I have ever heard. If I really believed all of that, I wouldn't be able to sleep. I would run down the streets screaming it to everyone. Why aren't you more excited about it?" That was a penetrating question.[4]

That is penetrating, isn't it? I remember a companion of mine who was moping about his girlfriend or something, and he walked about four or five feet behind me with his head down. Finally I asked him, "Elder, how do you think this looks to people when they see us walking by? Does it look like we're happy to be here, or does it look like drudgery?" (How's that for direct, honest, and clear?) We didn't run up and down the streets screaming, but we agreed to always radiate the message we had, even in the way we walked. President Spencer W. Kimball taught:

> Missionary conduct is noticed. You are known and recognized. You can't go into even a big town without being noticed. They see you in pairs and with books. They know you are ministers and they know you are Mormon missionaries and so the Church is what you show it to be. Someone may be watching you from a fourth-story window when you least expect it. And you are the Church to these people who know that you are members of it.[5]

I love President Kimball's words: *"You are the Church to these people!"* That realization helped my companion and me to always remember that those around us, including people we would never talk to, were forming their opinions about the Church and its message based on what they saw us do! Maybe in the future some elder or sister would approach someone who had seen us, and our behavior now might affect whether that person would listen then. That's a great responsibility!

I live in Provo, and sometimes I drive past the Missionary Training Center. Once I stopped my car some distance from the light to let some elders slip across the street without having to go clear down to the corner. I was a little disappointed that they crossed so slowly, without even acknowledging this patient driver who was waiting for them to get all the way across. Finally one of the last elders to cross looked at me and gave me a "thank-you" wave as he quickened his pace a little. I'm not worried about him, but I hope the rest of them learn that everything they do—yes, *everything*, even down to a little thing like crossing the street—leaves an impression. The world is watching our missionaries. You represent the Lord, his church, and 9.4 million others in the world. Represent us well!

Today, whenever anyone asks me about my mission companions, I just smile. (Okay, sometimes I bust out laughing.) We had wonderful times—too many and too varied to mention here. I don't see any of them very often anymore, but they are like brothers to me. I am grateful for my companions. I know that you will be grateful for yours, too—even the hard ones.

Missionary work is hard, but it would be much harder without a faithful companion. Thank goodness you don't have to be alone. And if you and your companion are different, that's okay; just be different together.

---

1. *Wall Street Journal*, May 4, 1988.

2. *The Teachings of Spencer W. Kimball* (Salt Lake City: Bookcraft, 1982), pp. 579–80.

3. *Teachings of Ezra Taft Benson* (Salt Lake City: Bookcraft, 1988), p. 203.

4. Glenn L. Pace, *Spiritual Plateaus* (Salt Lake City: Deseret Book, 1991), p. 46.

5. *The Teachings of Spencer W. Kimball*, p. 579.

Great Shall Be Your Joy

Many times you have desired of me to know that
which would be of the most worth unto you.
And now, behold, I say unto you, that the thing
which will be of the most worth unto you will be
to declare repentance unto this people, that you
may bring souls unto me, that you may
rest with them in the kingdom of
my Father. —D&C 15:4, 6

Now we come to the last member of the missionary trio "the Lord, my companion, and me." The Lord promises that your joy shall be great as you bring souls unto him (see D&C 18:15). He loves you as an individual. It was while I was on my mission that I learned that he really knew me and loved me. Before my mission, I *believed* he loved me, but I learned it on a much deeper level in the Philippines. I guess you could say I gained a testimony of it.

I was naive. I thought that while I was on my mission I would feel more righteous. The fact is, I probably was more righteous in my actions and attitudes. But I didn't feel it. What really happened to me was that I became more aware of my weaknesses. I had to confront the fact that I was often impatient, judgmental, selfish, prideful, materialistic, and so on. I guess you really start to notice those things when your mind is on the things of the Spirit all day long for two years.

I took comfort in the fact that even Nephi said, "O wretched man that I am" (2 Nephi 4:17). Wow. I wouldn't mind being "wretched" if that's what Nephi was. Nephi's sins were probably pretty minor, as sins go (he likely felt anger sometimes toward his brothers, for instance), but his spiritual awareness had increased to the point that even little things caused him great anxiety. I believe the same thing will happen to you on your mission. It's good for you. It keeps you humble. And you can either choose to be humble, or you can be compelled to be humble (see Alma 32:16).

I made mistakes on my mission; there were things I wish I hadn't done. They weren't sins so much as mistakes. I had been making mistakes all my life, though, so I don't know why I expected to stop making them on my mission.

One time I went to visit one of our less-active members a few hours before church on a Sunday morning. Sunday mornings can be hectic, and I was a little impatient. My companion that day was a deacon from the ward. When I came into the house, the man I had come to invite to church was drinking beer with his friends. I was visibly disappointed in him, and I said a few words I shouldn't have. I'm sure it embarrassed him in front of his friends. Oh, how I wish I could do that visit over again! It would have made such a difference if I had just ignored the beer and extended a loving hand of fellowship. What if I had smiled, said hello politely to his friends, and then invited him to church, as if I hadn't even seen the beer? Maybe it would have awakened his conscience. Why wasn't I smarter? Who appointed me Word of Wisdom Police anyway?

I never had a chance to apologize to that man. I have prayed very hard to be forgiven for that mistake. We're told to be bold, but not to be jerks—or, in other words, overbearing. Elder Neal A. Maxwell once said that today's *Missionary Handbook* could be compressed into these words of Alma: "Use boldness but not overbearance; and also see that ye bridle all your passions, that ye may be filled with love; see that ye refrain from idleness" (Alma 38:12).

Another time, as a young missionary, I had a rather heated debate with a completely inactive member who was a university professor. I wasn't very subtle. Gentle persuasion doesn't exactly imply verbally smacking people in the head with a two by four, which is about what happened. I knew that the spirit of contention was from the adversary, so why was I acting as if I didn't know it?

That was in my first area. I prayed for most of my mission that somehow I could go back and do that interaction over. But how could that ever happen? Whoever heard of a missionary serving in the same area twice?

Well, I believe the Lord loves his missionaries—even the ones who've made mistakes. Believe it or not, he heard my prayers, and I went back to that same area at the end of my mission. I got my chance to visit that man again, and I apologized. I confessed that I had been wrong, and then I did what I should've done in the first place—I told him I knew the Church was true, and that we all wanted him to come back to church. There was a much better spirit there. I don't know if that man will ever come back into activity. His peer group of professors had a very strong influence on him. But I thank my Heavenly Father that he let me go back to talk to him again.

Why am I telling you about my mistakes? Well, I want

you to know that you may make a few, even when you're doing the best you know how. Don't ever get the impression that once you're a missionary you've "arrived." "Proud missionary" is a contradiction in terms. Missionaries need the Atonement too. You need Jesus just as much as the people you are teaching do. Recognizing my weaknesses really softened my heart and helped me to see how much I needed the Lord.

I also want to assure you that if something is important to you, it's important to the Lord too. This was illustrated to me by another mistake I made on my mission.

I didn't talk to very many Americans in the Philippines, but one day when we were riding our bikes on Checkpoint Road, just south of Clark Air Force Base in Angeles City, an American on a motorcycle pulled alongside and started asking us questions. He asked if either of us was from Nevada. Elder Reidhead and I responded that we were from Arizona and Utah. We were pedaling along at a pretty constant rate, but he was having trouble matching our speed on his motorcycle. He'd hit the gas and pull ahead of us slightly, then coast until he was behind us again. We were watching and listening to him with our heads going back and forth like spectators at a tennis game. Finally he dropped further back than usual, and I thought he was going to turn off at an upcoming intersection. So I said, "Well, we'll see you later," and he glared at me as if to say, "Oh, you don't want to talk to me anymore, huh?" then he looked straight ahead, hit the gas, and sped away.

I felt horrible. Here I was, a representative of the Lord and the Church, and I had offended this man. As I reviewed our conversation, I realized that we had talked mostly about us. I felt so stupid. What had happened to all the things I had learned about dealing with people and making them feel valued and important? I know it was just a misunderstanding on my part, but I felt awful. I begged the Lord to let me see that man again, but I couldn't figure out how it could happen! I didn't even know what he looked like, because he had been wearing a helmet and all I could see were his eyes. Also, there were something like 50,000 Americans on that base—it was huge! For two weeks I prayed to find that motorcycle rider so I could make amends and change his impression about the Church. For me, it was the proverbial "needle in a haystack" situation. But the Lord knew exactly where he was.

One day, I was with Elder Comstock, my fellow zone leader, visiting the elders in a little town called Guagua. We were about forty-five minutes away from Angeles, Americans, or anything "stateside." Guagua is the *real* Philippines—no souvenir stores, tourist sites, or night clubs for American servicemen. After our visit, we went to the bus station to catch the next "Philippine Rabbit" back to Angeles. We were late, and the schedule said we had missed it. But as we walked outside, we saw the bus come around the corner. The doors opened and we stepped onto the bus, only to see that it was full. The only seats available were back by the engine, where it was even hotter than it was outside. As we walked down the aisle, I noticed four American servicemen in the back seats. We sat next to them because there weren't any other available seats in the whole bus. After a minute or two, one of the servicemen looked at us and said, "What I wanna know is why you guys won't serve in the military." I explained that he had us mixed up with another religion, and showed him calling cards from some of the LDS officers on the base. Just then, the guy next to him sat forward and said, "I talked to some of you guys the other day."

I couldn't believe my ears. Wide-eyed, I said, "Where?"

"In Angeles," he responded.

"Were you on a motorcycle?" I asked.

"Yeah."

"THAT WAS YOU!?" I blurted out with barely concealed enthusiasm. "I mean, uh, that was you?"

"Yup," he said.

I could not believe it. It was the same man I had talked to more than two weeks earlier in Elder Reidhead's area. Not only did the Lord help me find him, He put me right next to him in the only available seat on the bus, and he wasn't going anywhere for forty-five minutes. I focused on him; I talked about the Church; I talked his ear off, in fact, and made sure I left him with a good impression.

I wish I could say that he's now a bishop or something, but actually, he wasn't the least bit interested in hearing about the Church. To me, that makes the story that much more interesting. The Lord knew that this man did not want to talk to the missionaries at all, but he also knew that it was very important to Elder Bytheway to meet this man again. And he arranged it.

Every time I recall that event, it amazes me. I've relied on that experience since, especially when I was having trouble finding someone who would marry me. I knew that the Lord could get two people in the same place at the same time without taking away the agency of either one. And he did that for me. Oh yes, the Lord can find needles in a haystack, and that means that he can also find the people that you have the particular talents to teach.

This experience taught me that the Lord really loves us and is involved in every aspect of our lives if we will let him be. President John Taylor once said, "God lives, and his eyes are over us, and his angels are round and about us, and they are more interested in us than we are in ourselves, ten thousand times, but we do not know it."[1]

I love the Lord Jesus Christ. I grew closer to him on my mission than I imagined was possible—and every time I grew closer to him, I wanted to tell more people about him. I wanted to tell them how he lived, what he taught, and how he died, not only for our sins but also for our mistakes and, yes, for the mistakes of missionaries too.

Why did I serve a mission? Well, my mission was for people in the Philippines who are now members of the Church, but I think it was also for me. I am so glad I went! Are you beginning to see why people say the time they spend on their missions is the best two years of their lives?

Before I end this section, I want to say some more about your testimony. When I first went into the MTC, I guess I thought a testimony was something you got, like a bicycle, and once you had it, it was always there. Now I believe a testimony is more like a garden, something you have to maintain. In order to produce fruit or vegetables or flowers, a garden must be tended and nurtured *daily*. It must be weeded regularly, or it will be overcome. When properly cared for, a testimony, like a garden, grows. The growth can be so small that you don't notice it. You may have days on your mission when you wish your testimony was stronger. In reality, because the process is so gradual, you might not recognize how much it has really grown.

A testimony also requires faith. You plant the seeds and you exercise faith that they will grow. The world often operates on the premise, "Seeing is believing." But a testimony is the other way around: *"Believing is seeing."* You must believe, and act, and then you'll see. Look at Ether 3:9: "And the Lord said unto him: Because of thy faith, thou hast seen . . . " You don't stand in front of a fireplace and say, "Give me heat, and then I'll give you wood." That's backwards. You do the work, you put the wood in first, and then the heat comes. The Lord requires that we move and act in faith, and he will bless us with growth and a stronger testimony.

As with a garden, you have to put some things into a testimony before you can get anything out. In other words, *you can't teach things you don't know about.* This is why you've been encouraged to read and study the scriptures all your life. If all those ideas are back in your brain, the Lord can help you retrieve them. But if you've never put them there in the first place, you can't get them out. As the scripture suggests, "Neither take ye thought beforehand what ye shall say; but *treasure up in your minds continually the words of life,* and it shall be given you in the very hour that portion that shall be meted unto every man" (D&C 84:85; emphasis added).

The more I learn, the more I can bring into my prayers when I ask, "Is this true?" Therefore, the more I do my daily scripture study, the more I understand about the gospel. And the more I understand about the gospel, the more things I can ask the Lord to confirm in my heart. Again, you can't teach what you haven't already learned— I can't tell someone about Nephi if I've never heard of him. Your gospel study time is set aside for a reason. What a luxury! Later in life, you will wish you had two hours a day for gospel study, I guarantee it. Take advantage of it! Get into it! Become acquainted with the scriptures and the prophets! Do your gospel study so that your testimony can grow and you can be a more useful instrument in the Lord's hands.

The Lord has amazing things to teach you on your mission: things about yourself, things about the gospel, and things about him. "Be thou humble; and the Lord thy God shall lead thee by the hand, and give thee answer to thy prayers" (D&C 112:10).

I loved my mission. It stretched my soul in a hundred

different ways. There were times when I was riding my bike home after a night of teaching that I thought my heart would burst with joy. Sometimes, as I pedaled along with a nighttime tropical breeze in my face, I thought about how blessed I was to know what I knew. Why was I so lucky? Why did I get the chance to know about Nephi and Ammon and Moroni from my youth? My mission wasn't a sacrifice, it was the least I could do! At times I couldn't understand why my blessings were so great, but I was truly grateful, and I'd look up in the night sky at that beautiful display of stars and feel that Heavenly Father was right there watching his young sons pedal home. When we put our whole heart and soul into our work, I even felt that he was smiling upon us. Inside our apartment, I'd kneel by my bed and say, "I love thee, Father. I love what I'm learning, and I love what I'm feeling. I'm so honored to be thy son. I'm so honored to be a missionary."

When I ripped open my mission call those many months ago, I read too quickly the words that were now coming true: "Greater blessings and more happiness than you have yet experienced await you as you humbly and prayerfully serve the Lord in this labor of love among his children." Elder, Sister, whoever you are, may you experience this happiness, and the great joy promised in the scriptures: "And if it so be that you should labor all your days in crying repentance unto this people, and bring, save it be one soul unto me, how great shall be your joy with him in the kingdom of my Father!" (D&C 18:15).

I hope you have felt the Spirit tug at your heart as you have read this book, and that you're anxious to get into your field of labor and be the best missionary you can be. I hope you will have a successful mission. I hope you will feel the joy of knowing you are exactly where the Lord wants you to be. I hope you will feel the Holy Ghost burn within you as you bear your testimony. I hope that "the Lord, your companion, and you" will have a wonderful adventure together. Souls are out there waiting for you and me, my friend. So "thrust in your sickle with all your might," and I look forward to rejoicing with them and with you on that glorious day!

---

1. In *Journal of Discourses,* 26 vols. (London: Latter-day Saints' Book Depot, 1856-86), 23:221-22.

Appendix:
Notes on the Apostasy, Reformation, and Restoration

We don't ask people to throw away any good that
they have got; we only ask them to come
and get more. —Joseph Smith

This is an appendix. I know it looks like a page in a book, but actually, it's an appendix. Have you ever seen an appendix? Me neither. I only know you should remove it if it hurts. An appendix is something that we know is there, but we don't know what it's for.

In the world of books and publishing, however, an appendix is something extra, something added to the main stuff because the author thought it might be important. Well, I'm the author and I do think it's important. Now it's my job to try to convince *you* that it's important so that you'll read it.

When I was a prospective missionary, I wasn't particularly interested in learning about these events. You may scan these next few pages and feel the same way. That's okay. I understand, because when I was in your position, the part of me that loves this stuff was still asleep. It woke up later on my mission. That part of you will wake up too. You see, when you wear that name badge, and you tell people you're a missionary, they figure you're some kind of an expert on religion. People start asking you questions, if you can imagine such a thing. Here are some typical ones:

Hasn't Christianity been on the earth all along?

Why is the LDS view of God so different from traditional Christianity?

Why should I be baptized again?

Why did the Romans adopt Christianity?

Do Latter-day Saints accept the doctrine of Trinity?

Isn't it more holy not to get married?

Doesn't the Bible say you can't have any new scripture?

What happened in all those years between A.D. *300 and 1000?*

Where did the Greek Orthodox Church come from?

Hasn't Christianity been the cause of more wars and bloodshed than any other religion?

Were people reading the scriptures through the centuries?

Why a Restoration? Wasn't the Reformation enough?

Why would God choose to restore the church in America?

Well, there are answers to those questions. But be careful—as we've already learned, the Spirit is what converts, not clever arguments or a barrage of information. I included this part because it has been very helpful for *me*. I hope it will be helpful for you too.

The answers to the questions above, and many, many others, are found in the study of the Apostasy, the Reformation, and the Restoration. When I entered the MTC, I knew a little bit about the Apostasy. I knew the prophecies about a "famine of hearing the words of the

Lord" (Amos 8:11). I knew that Peter spoke of the "restitution of all things," and that Paul taught that Jesus would not come until there was a "falling away first" (Acts 3:20–21; 2 Thessalonians 2:2–3). I learned more during my mission as I studied *A Marvelous Work and a Wonder*, and I learned what I could from other missionaries. I got intensely curious! But alas, my dad's fine library was home in Utah. When I returned from the Philippines, I really began to search and study, and, well, I wish I had known this before I served my mission!

You, future missionary, have recently arrived on the scene of a big mess. You were saved to come forth in the latter days, and now you're smack-dab in the middle of this chaos called Planet Earth in the late twentieth century. You've seen the mess on the evening news, and you feel like asking, what on earth happened!?

Today, some baptize by immersion, others by sprinkling; still others say baptism is unnecessary. Some religions have a paid ministry, some have lay clergy, some simply broadcast their meetings over the television to people in their homes. Some are absolutely adamant about the Sabbath being on Saturday, and others are sure that only 144,000 will go to heaven. Some believe in tithing, some pass the plate, and others give you a 1–800 number and let you donate by Visa or MasterCard. What happened to the simple but profound ministry of Jesus Christ? How did the church go from one unified body to more than 1600 different Christian denominations today?

HISTORY IS NOT PRETTY

In high school, while preparing for history tests, someone would always ask the teacher in a whiney tone, "Do we have to know the dates?" At that time, I wanted to *go on* dates, not *memorize* them. But now I know the value of understanding what happened, why and how it happened,

and yup, even *when* it happened. As we look at history, we
see the church that Jesus organized dwindle and die, we
see his basic doctrines being corrupted or changed, and we
also see the growing necessity for a complete restoration.
This helps us better understand our own small role in the
Restoration as missionaries and messengers of the good
news of the gospel. I love it, and I'm not a whiner about
dates anymore.

Question: Hasn't Christianity been on the earth all along?

*Answer: In one form or another, yes. But not as Jesus orga-
nized it. So-called "traditional Christianity" bears little resem-
blance to the ancient Christian church and beliefs. Read on:*

A.D. 30: As you know, during his lifetime Jesus established his church on the earth. He was betrayed by Judas,
taken, and crucified. After Judas committed suicide, the
apostles met to fill the vacancy in the Twelve (see Acts
1:24–26). Matthias was chosen to replace Judas.
Apparently the organization of the Twelve Apostles was
meant to continue.

A.D. 33–101: The resurrected Jesus gave the apostles the
charge, "Go ye into all the world, and preach the gospel to
every creature" (Mark 16:15). They taught faith and repentance in Jesus Christ, baptized people by immersion, and
gave the gift of the Holy Ghost. By about 101 A.D., all of the
apostles were gone. Tradition holds that most of them
were martyred, while John the Beloved was banished to
the Isle of Patmos in 101 A.D. We know that John the
Beloved has been on the earth ever since. But the Church
was now left without proper leadership and priesthood
direction. We'll see more of the effects of this breakdown
in priesthood leadership as we continue.

*Question: Why is the LDS view of God so different from tra-
ditional Christianity?*

Answer: Christianity adopted much of Greek philosophy into its teaching, and the original concept of God was changed. Keep reading!

A.D. 100–200: During the second century, Greek philosophy, particularly the work of Plato, was the currently accepted belief among the ruling class. The Christians were persecuted and criticized in part because their teachings were not enough like Plato's teachings. Plato taught that God was incomprehensible to men and completely unlike man in every way, whereas the Christians (at least the ancient Christians) believed the words of the prophets, who taught that God has a body and that we are created in his image. It's interesting to see what an anti-Christian writer of the day had to say about the Christian teachings in about A.D. 178.

> The Christians say that God has hands, a mouth, and a voice; they are always proclaiming that "God said this" or "God spoke." "The heavens declare the work of his hands," they say. I can only comment that such a God is no god at all, for God has neither hands, mouth, or voice, nor any characteristics of which we know. And they say that God made man in his own image, failing to realize that God is not at all like a man, nor vice versa; God resembles no form known to us. They say that God has form, namely the form of the Logos, who became flesh in Jesus Christ. But we know that God is without shape, without color. They say that God moved above the waters he created—but we know that it is contrary to the nature of God to move. Their absurd doctrines even contain references to God walking about in the garden he created for man; and they speak of him being angry, jealous, moved to repentance, sorry, sleepy—in short, as being in every respect more a man than a God. They have not read Plato, who teaches us in the *Republic,*

that God (the Good) does not even participate in being.[1]

This is amazing. Here was a follower of Plato criticizing the early Christians for the same things the Latter-day Saints are often criticized about today. He ridiculed them for believing what the prophets said about God: that he has a body and that we are created in his image! What a difference a millennium makes!

What happened in the years that followed is referred to by historians as the "Hellenization of Christianity." (*Hellenization* refers to the merging of Greek thought and culture with one's own beliefs and practices.) In order to win respect and acceptance from those in the Graeco-Roman world, some Christians sought to defend Christianity using Greek philosophy. The ideas that Plato held about God suddenly became more important than what Christ taught. As one writer put it, "It may well be said of Plato that he had a greater influence in forming the traditional concept of God than Christ himself."[2]

Without the priesthood leadership and revelation for the church, the "falling away" predicted by Paul had begun. The apostles were unable to meet and fill the vacancies in the Twelve as they had done before. Bishops (*local* authorities) of the many cities were left without the priesthood supervision of the apostles (*general* authorities). False teachers and false doctrines arose. An ancient historian named Eusebius (A.D. 260–339) wrote:

> The Church continued until then [close of the first century] as a pure and uncorrupt virgin, whilst if there were any at all that attempted to pervert the sound doctrine of the saving gospel, they were yet skulking in dark retreats: but *when the sacred choir of Apostles became extinct* and the generation of those that had been privileged to hear their inspired wisdom had

passed away, then also the *combinations of impious errors arose* by the fraud and delusions of false teachers. These also as there were none of the apostles left, henceforth attempted without shame, to preach their *false doctrines against the gospel truth.*[3]

Why is our view of God different from that of traditional Christianity? Well, obviously, what the adversary would want to do is change God from a personal, loving Father in Heaven to an unknowable, incomprehensible spirit creature who is without body, parts, or passions.

Question: Why should I be baptized again?

Answer: Baptism must be performed by one with priesthood authority, and it must be done by immersion.

A.D. 300–350: It is recorded that Cyprian, the learned Bishop of Carthage (North Africa), baptized someone by sprinkling instead of immersion because the person being baptized had some physical weakness. The practice became widespread in the years to come. Later, Saint Augustine (A.D. 354–430) preached the doctrine of original sin. In order to erase the taint of original sin as soon as possible, the practice of baptizing infants was begun.

Question: Why did the Romans adopt Christianity?

Answer: They didn't at first. The early Christians endured horrible persecutions.

A.D. 284–305: Diocletian was the emperor of Rome. Horrible, government-sponsored persecutions forced the Christians underground (literally, into the catacombs beneath Rome). The empire confiscated the existing scriptures, imprisoned and tortured the clergy, and forced Christians to worship pagan gods or face death. It was a horrible time, and many Christians died as martyrs.

Question: Do Latter-day Saints accept the doctrine of Trinity?

Answer: We accept the teaching that the Father and the Son are one, but only in purpose. Each of us hopes to be "one with them" someday, as Jesus prayed we would (see John 17:21).

A.D. 325: Persecutions persisted, but Christianity would not go away. After eliminating his rivals, Emperor Constantine saw an advantage in supporting Christianity (after seeing a vision of a glowing cross with the message "by this conquer"), but he was having trouble keeping the peace. He felt that if he could unite the Christian factions, he could stabilize his empire. A council of bishops was convened in Nicaea in Bithyria, Asia Minor. One of the items on the agenda was to settle the ongoing disagreement about the nature of God. Were the Father and the Son one in purpose or one in person? Did Jesus Christ really possess a body of flesh and bone after his resurrection, or should a man-made philosophy prevail? After spirited debate, the assembled bishops came up with a document or a "creed." Some of the bishops signed it even though they disagreed—at least the persecutions were over and there was peace in the empire. The document this council produced is commonly known as the Nicene Creed. In it, the doctrine of the Trinity—three Gods in one—emerged (another victory for Greek philosophy). Because Emperor Constantine presided over this whole affair, the church now became a "state" church, or, in other words, the state now had power in church matters. Constantine's effort to unite the church was successful, and this new church would later be known as the universal or "Catholic" church.

There are three reasons why this is such an important event to mention. First, it shows how decision making in the church had changed. The way to settle doctrinal questions was not to go to the Lord's prophet and seek revelation, but to get together and debate and vote and try to figure things out with man's reason. Second, it marks the official acceptance of the man-made doctrine of the Trinity. Third, it is the beginning of a state-controlled church, a horrible precedent. (The founding fathers were adamant about separation of church and state, because they had witnessed several centuries of abuses from a state church.)

Question: Isn't it more holy not to get married?

Answer: Marriage is ordained of God and is part of becoming more like God.

Once the church concluded that God didn't have a body or parts or passions, the natural next step was to assume that man's body, parts, and passions must be bad. This idea is called asceticism. Although Jesus (see Mark 10:7–9) and Paul (see Hebrews 13:4) had taught that marriage was honorable, it was determined that in order to be closest to God, you shouldn't marry. Celibacy had been practiced by many people for many reasons; it's impossible to put a date on when it began as an official practice of the church, but it is considered a part of the Great Apostasy. Obviously, because marriage is a step toward eternal life, Satan will do all he can to prevent it. Paul commented that "in the latter times some shall depart from the faith, giving heed to seducing spirits, and doctrines of devils; Speaking lies in hypocrisy; having their conscience seared with a hot iron; Forbidding to marry . . ." (1 Timothy 4:3). Thus the doctrine of eternal marriage, or the "new and everlasting covenant," was destroyed.

Question: Doesn't the Bible say you can't have any new scripture?

Answer: Revelation 22:18 contains a warning not to add to "this book," but so does Deuteronomy 4:2. Also, the Bible (a word that means "books") wasn't even assembled as one book until well into the fourth century. It's also generally accepted that the epistles of John were written after the book of

Revelation. We believe these warnings were about individual books or revelations, and not about the Bible, which wasn't even a book when they were given. (Also, John 21:25 tells us that the world itself could not contain the books of all the things that Jesus did.)

A.D. 363–397: "By the fourth century precisely what was 'official scripture' was finally decided. Athanasius (A.D. 293–373), the bishop of Alexandria, publicly listed as authoritative scripture the same twenty-seven books we have in our present New Testament. . . . The list which Athanasius drew up was also accepted as canonical (though not without debate) by the majority of those church leaders present at the councils of Laodicea (A.D. 363), Hippo (A.D. 393), and Carthage (A.D. 397)."[4]

Question: What happened in all those years between A.D. 300 and 1000?

Answer: Lots of things—too many, in fact, to include for our purposes, but here's a little bit.

The Catholic church was essentially the only Christian church in existence for several centuries, its history characterized by power struggles, intrigue, and heresy. A historian describing these years said:

> It seemed impossible that things could become worse; yet Rome had still to see Benedict IX, A.D. 1033, a boy of less than twelve years, raised to the apostolic throne. Of this pontiff, one of his successors, Victor III, declared that his life was so shameful, so foul, so execrable, that he shuddered to describe it. He ruled like a captain of banditti rather than a prelate. The people at last, unable to bear his adulteries, homicides and abominations any longer, rose up against him. In despair of maintaining his position, he put up the papacy to auction. It was bought by a presbyter named John, who became Gregory VI, A.D. 1045.[5]

More basic doctrines were altered. Instead of a worship service in which the members participated, the mass became more of a performance, with much pomp, mystery, and ceremony.

Question: Where did the Greek Orthodox church come from?

Answer: This was the first major split of the church, and it happened in A.D. 1054.

The Roman church filled Europe but was ruled from Rome. The church had changed from a persecut*ed* church to a persecut*ing* church. Those who disagreed with its doctrines or practices were called heretics, and they were usually tortured and killed. Is it any wonder that these many centuries when the "Light of the World" was gone are referred to as the "Dark Ages"?

A.D. 1054: A centuries-old rivalry concerning the location from which the church should be governed resulted in the split of the church into the Roman Catholic church, with headquarters in Rome, and the Greek Orthodox church, with headquarters in Constantinople, Greece. (Constantinople is now Istanbul.)

Question: Hasn't Christianity been the cause of more wars and bloodshed than any other religion?

Answer: This is probably true, largely because of the Crusades and the Inquisition. But the real issue is not what Christianity did to man, it's what man did to Christianity. This is further evidence that the gospel of peace and of the golden rule was long gone.

A.D. 1096–1204: The Crusades were military expeditions intended to take the Holy Land from the Muslims. Unfortunately, they hardened Muslim attitudes toward Christians, and those attitudes remain today.

A.D. 1129–1834: The Inquisition was a Roman Catholic tribunal whose purpose was to seek out and prosecute heretics. The accused were often tortured into confessing and then killed. Joan of Arc was a victim of the Inquisition. The Inquisition was an example of the barbarism of the Middle Ages, and it is an embarrassment to modern Christians.

Question: Were people reading the scriptures through the centuries?

Answer: No. Only the clergy had access to scriptures, and they were in Hebrew and Greek. St. Jerome translated existing manuscripts into Latin, the common or "vulgar" language, in A.D. *405. This translation is called the "Vulgate." But until the invention of the printing press in the 1400s, scriptures had to be copied by hand and thus were very rare.*

A.D. 1160: Where's Waldo? The peasant classes were uneducated and without the blessings of the scriptures for centuries. A merchant named Waldo hired a monk to translate portions of the scriptures into his language. Waldo went about preaching in secret; his followers were called the Waldenses. George Albert Smith reported: "They were severely persecuted by the Catholic Church, which anathematized them and inflicted upon them every penalty in its power—even excommunication, sword and fire. Notwithstanding all this the Waldenses progressed, and their doctrines and the work they performed was a nursery for the Reformation."[6]

A.D. 1380–1388: John Wycliffe's Bible was brought forth as the first English translation of the scriptures. Because a knowledge of the scriptures tended to increase people's dissatisfaction with the church, the church strongly discouraged reading them, reserving that right for the clergy only. We remember John Wycliffe with honor, but Lenet Hadley Read reports: "An epitaph written at St. Albans called Wycliffe 'The devil's instrument, church's enemy, people's confusion, heretic's idol, hypocrite's mirror, schism's broacher, hatred's sower, lies' forger, flatteries' sink, who, stricken by the horrible judgements of God, breathed forth his soul to the dark mansion of the black devil.'" Believe it or not, the hatred toward Wycliffe grew to the point that in later years people dug up his body from where it was buried, burned it, and threw the ashes into a river.[7]

A.D. 1440: Very few copies of the scriptures were in existence. Books had to be hand copied and were very expensive. It would cost you a wagon load of hay to rent the New Testament for one day. In about 1440, the printing press came into existence. This meant that copies of the scriptures would be more available to everyone. The church was violently opposed to the development of printing. Elder Bruce R. McConkie states:

> Few tools were more effective than printing in paving the way for the great revival of learning, for the religious reformation, and for the breaking away of peoples and nations from religious domination. Without the discovery of movable type in about 1440 A.D. the barrier of gross darkness covering the apostate world could scarce have been pierced. One of the first books published was the Gutenberg Bible in 1456 A.D.
>
> Perhaps no important discovery in world history ever faced such intense and bitter opposition as arose over the use and spread of printing. Civil and ecclesiastical tyrants feared the loss of their ill-held and evilly-exercised powers should knowledge and truth be made available to people generally. "We must root out printing," said the Vicar of Croydon from his pulpit, "or printing will root us out."[8]

Despite the opposition, printing flourished, and the scriptures were read by an ever-increasing number. There was a great revival of learning and of the arts, and this period marks the end of the Dark Ages and is often called the Renaissance.

A.D. 1492: Now we begin to see the hand of the Lord preparing the "restitution of all things" spoken of by Peter. In 1492, Christopher Columbus set off to find a shorter route to India. This event is prophesied in the Book of Mormon (see 1 Nephi 13:12).

Question: Why a Restoration? Wasn't the Reformation enough?

Answer: No. We believe the reformers were noble men with a portion of the Spirit of God, but only God himself could restore the lost priesthood authority. The problem is, although the reformers moved closer to teachings of the original church, they took much of the baggage of traditional Christianity with them.

A.D. 1517: A monk and university professor named Martin Luther became concerned about certain abuses and practices of the Catholic church. In 1517, he prepared a list of 95 theses (subjects for debate) and nailed them to the door of the All Saints Church in Wittenberg, Germany.

The church did not appreciate Luther's dissension, and eventually he was forced into hiding. Luther had friends in high places or he probably would have been killed, as were many others who protested against the church. Luther continued to write while he was in hiding. Some agreed with Luther; others opposed him. King Henry VIII of England sided with the church and published a book in its defense for which he was awarded the title "Defender of the Faith," a title still carried by British kings.

Luther gained a following, and his movement eventually resulted in the formation of a "new" church called the Lutheran church. Martin Luther is recognized as the first "Protestant," and his movement marks the beginning of the Reformation. But it was not Luther's original intent to form a new church. He said: "I have sought nothing beyond reforming the Church in conformity with the Holy Scriptures. The spiritual powers have been not only corrupted by sin, but absolutely destroyed; so that there is now nothing in them but a depraved reason and a will that is the enemy and opponent of God. I simply say that Christianity has ceased to exist among those who should have preserved it."[9]

A.D. 1535: Tension had been mounting for some time between the church in Rome and the governments of some European nations. A portion of the taxes collected by these governments was sent to Rome. Tensions reached a peak in England when, in 1529, Henry VIII desired a divorce from his wife, Catherine of Aragon. The pope would not grant this divorce, and in 1535, parliament declared Henry VIII the supreme head of the church in England. Thus, Henry VIII became head of both church and state in England, giving him the authority to grant his own divorce. Some refused to recognize this action, and Henry had many of them executed. Ties with the Roman Catholic church were formally broken, and the Church of England—also called the Anglican and, in America, the Episcopalian church—was born.

A.D. 1609: Another group, observing from the Bible that baptism was performed only on those capable of repenting, were eventually formed into a church by John Smith in 1609. This group performed baptisms first by pouring and later by immersion. Others referred to them as "Anabaptists" or rebaptizers. Persecutions raged against them, and many Anabaptists were publicly drowned. The Anabaptists were the beginning of the Baptist movement.

A.D. 1620: Just eleven years later, in 1620, the *Mayflower* set sail for America, its passengers in search of religious freedom. Seven ancestors of Joseph Smith were on board.

A.D. 1639: In Providence, Rhode Island, a Puritan minister named Roger Williams founded the first Baptist church in America. In this remarkable statement, we see that Williams knew that a *Reformation* was not enough—a *Restoration* was needed: "There is no regularly constituted church on earth, nor any person qualified to administer any church ordinances; nor can there be until new apostles are sent by the Great Head of the Church for whose coming I am seeking."[10]

A.D. 1649: John Calvin and John Knox were the forces behind the Protestant movement called Presbyterianism, which was formed about 1649. The word *Presbyterian* refers to a representative form of church government. In Greek, *presbyteros* means "elder."[11] Calvin and Knox formed a church government similar to that which was practiced in the first century.

A.D. 1738: John and Charles Wesley were brothers who attended Oxford University in England. They formed the "Holy Club," but were nicknamed "Methodists" by the student body because of their strict and methodical rules of conduct and religious observance. John Wesley did not intend to organize a new sect, but gained many followers after he began to preach in about 1738. The first Methodist church in America was formally established in 1784.[12] How did John Wesley feel about traditional Christianity?

> It does not appear that these extraordinary gifts of the Holy Ghost were common in the Church for more than two or three centuries. We seldom hear of them after that fatal period when the Emperor Constantine called himself a Christian. . . . From this time they almost totally ceased. . . . The Christians had no more of the Spirit of Christ than the other heathens. . . . This was the real cause why the extraordinary gifts of the Holy Ghost were no longer to be found in the Christian Church; because the Christians

were turned heathen again, and had only a dead form left.[13]

Question: Why would God choose to restore the church in America? (I heard this one a lot on my mission.)

Answer: Perhaps one reason is that the United States was the first country to guarantee religious freedom.

A.D. 1776: The Declaration of Independence was signed, and America was thrust into the Revolutionary War. In 1791 the Bill of Rights was finally ratified, guaranteeing among other things the free exercise of religion. People had been coming to America since the time of the pilgrims to enjoy freedom of worship. Now that freedom was guaranteed, and the time was perfect for a complete restoration of the gospel.

One of the signers of the Declaration of Independence, and one of our founding fathers, was Thomas Jefferson. Here is what he had to say about religion:

> The religion builders have so distorted and deformed the doctrines of Jesus, so muffled them in mysticisms, fancies and falsehoods, have caricatured them into forms so inconceivable, as to shock reasonable thinkers. . . . Happy in the prospect of a *restoration* of primitive Christianity, I must leave to younger persons to encounter and lop off the false branches which have been engrafted into it by the mythologists of the middle and modern ages.[14]

A.D. 1805: Just fourteen years after the Constitution was ratified, Joseph Smith was born in Sharon, Vermont. There is not room to retell his story here; I hope you will stop at this point and read it for yourself in Joseph Smith—History in the Pearl of Great Price.

A.D. 1820: Joseph Smith described the events that led him to pray for guidance: